EVIL'S GREAT MASQUERADE:
DIVINE LIGHT OR DECEPTIVE WOO?

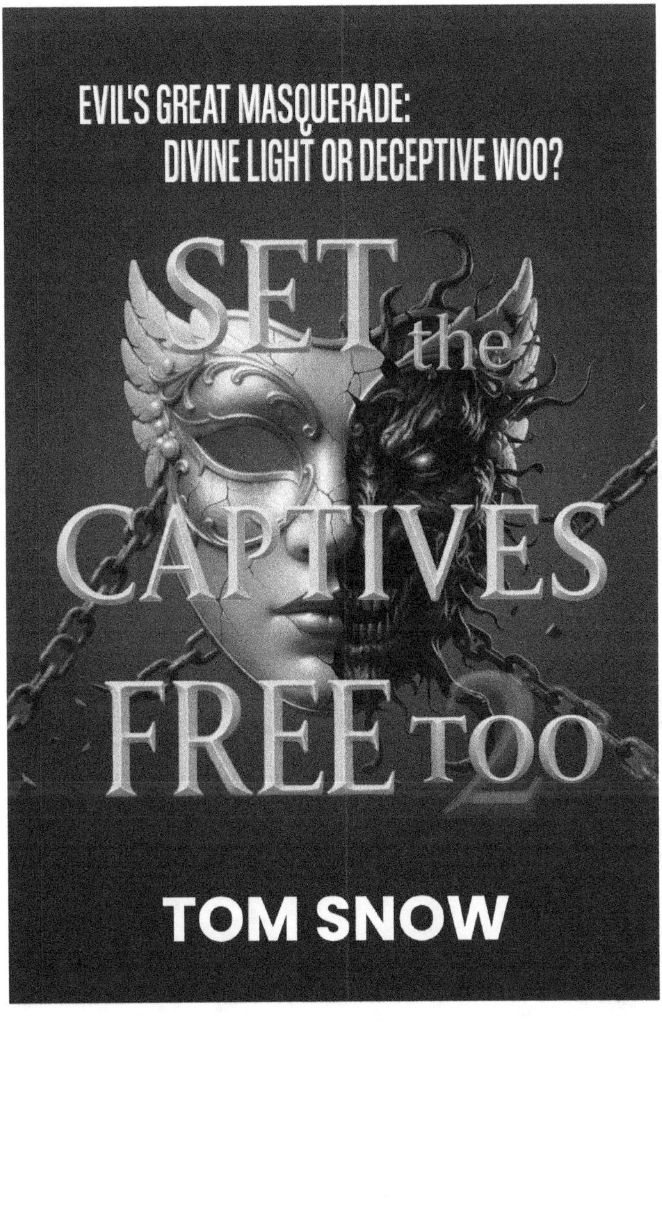

SET the CAPTIVES FREE too

TOM SNOW

Set the Captives Free Too

Evil's Great Masquerade: Divine Light or Deceptive Woo?

Tom Snow

JUST TO BE CLEAR TEACHING SERIES

Light, Truth, Blood

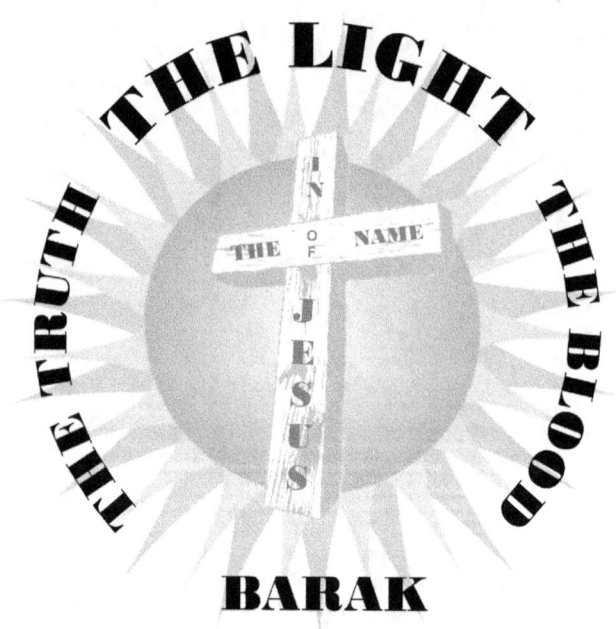

THE LIGHT

THE TRUTH

THE BLOOD

IN THE NAME OF JESUS

BARAK

DEDICATION

I DEDICATE THIS BOOK to the Lord Jesus Christ, the Holy Spirit, and Papa God, the Father.

I also dedicate it to my wonderful wife, Danielle, and my daughter Juliette, who likewise love the Lord.

I want to mention and do some shout-outs to Morgane Rose, who openly shared her testimony for all of us in Chapter One. Along with all my good friends who gave valuable feedback as I wrote this book, with a special shout-out to Ashley who always asks a "million" questions and challenges me in the best way.

As well as there are other people who I will NOT mention by name who are currently going down their own paths in Woo and haven't come back to the Light. Each has had an unknowing input into this writing, as their plight has saddened my heart. I address the deceptions they're still living in throughout this book, mentioning no one in particular. I pray for their very best as they navigate the darkness and for them to come back into Papa's loving arms.

CONTENTS

NOTES

SOURCES

VERSES OR VERSE FRAGMENTS originate from the New American Standard Version Bible (NASB)®, New International Version Bible (NIV)®, The Amplified Bible (AMP)®, The King James Version Bible (KJV)®, or Strong's® Greek and Hebrew original texts; citations may or may not be included. All other names, trademarks, and any other such rights are owned by their respective originators. All other rights are reserved.

FORWARD

BETWEEN GOOD AND EVIL

Central to Understanding the Battle for Our Minds:

"AND NO WONDER, FOR Satan himself **masquerades [disguises]** as an **angel of light**. It is not surprising, then, if his servants also **masquerade [disguise]** as **servants of righteousness**." (2 Corinthians 11:14-15)

The word **masquerades [or disguises]** in the Greek is 'metaschēmatizō' and means, "to give a certain form to something," "to change in fashion or appearance," "disguise," "disguises," "disguising," and "transform."

"BELOVED, **do not put faith in** and **believe every spirit**, but **prove (test) the spirits** to discover whether they proceed from God." (1 John 4:1)

"**Be alert** and **of sober mind** [vigilant and cautious] at all times. Because **your enemy** [adversary], **the devil**, prowls [roams] around like a roaring lion **looking for someone to seize upon** and **devour**." (1 Peter 5:8)

If you don't understand how important these verses are, blindness may have already occurred, and nothing else in this book will make sense.

INTRODUCTION

MY PLANS

I HAD (FINALLY) HOPED to write ***BREAKING THE CURSE OF THE GENERATIONS*** next, but the Lord had a different idea.

Note: In the toss-up, He wins every time!

Instead, I'm writing a follow-up to the last book, ***SET THE CAPTIVES FREE***. That book dealt with very serious subjects holding God's people captive in the churches, religions, and denominations by false Belief Systems, spiritual Stockholm Syndrome and "Egypt in the Church."

This book goes far beyond that to address the vast number of wrong / false "spiritual things" going on in the world, permeating the Church, and hurting many.

THIS BOOK WILL BE WORTH YOUR TIME

Some chapters in this book may seem long, yet they are essential in discussing the many false spiritual deceptions affecting many, many people in the world and in the churches today.

Every chapter has a strong purpose, which builds upon the last, so you can learn **ALL** you need to know in fighting a vast **UNSEEN WORLD**.

With so many critically important subjects covered in this book, I guarantee you it's going to be worth your while. They are critical to the physical, mental, emotional, and spiritual health of **ALL**.

By the time you finish reading, you'll either thank me or hate me.

Either way, you won't be able to say nobody warned you.

The Masking   The Un-Masking

QUOTES FROM EARLY READERS

"PART TESTIMONY, PART EVIDENCE, all leading to ONE Truth. Where the Bible, science and human experience all prove the real danger of woo and that Jesus is the ONLY way. For believers, non-believers, and everyone seeking answers."

"This book was not an easy read—and I mean that in the best way possible. It challenged my assumptions, pushed me to think deeper, and forced me to confront ideas I had accepted without question. The writing is direct, honest, and unafraid to go where many authors won't. Whether you agree with every point or not, this book will absolutely make you stop and think. A bold and timely message for the world we're living in."

"I have been waiting for a book like this; I have never read anything like it!"

"This book is an in-your-face, unapologetic wake-up call to those who've been seduced and 'wooed' by the enemy's never-ending, smooth-talked destructive lies, and an extensive resource for those who are doing the Lord's work to help open the eyes of the blind."

"This book has great stories, applications, Biblical references, and teaching points that have educated and equipped me on the up and coming woo deception!"

"Insightful, intriguing, revelatory, and extremely eye opening!"

"This book showed me things that have been right under my nose and taught me how to have eyes to see and ears to hear with the various ways the enemy has crept into our culture and even our church."

"This is not just a book; this is a spiritual warfare and woo manual that is going on my resources shelf!"

"As someone in full time ministry, this is a must read for all Christians including pastors, those on the mission field, Christian therapists, and anyone else serving the Lord in any capacity!"

"This book has great Biblical responses (literal Scripture) to help combat various woo and New Age comments. I will be highlighting these verses in my Bible!"

"A must read for all Christians; you may think you know about the New Age movement and woo deception, but this book will only widen your knowledge of it and equip you with deeper understanding of how to handle the occult that has truly mascaraed itself."

"This book doesn't just identify the problem—it names the source, exposes the method, and provides the exit. Most books do one. This does all three."

"The two-source framework is devastatingly simple: if it's not from God, there's only one other option. Once you see it, you can't unsee it."

"Chapter 14 answers the question everyone asks but no one explains: why do psychics seem accurate? The answer is more disturbing—and more logical—than I expected."

"The sarcasm isn't cruelty—it's clarity. Sometimes the most loving thing you can do is stop being polite about poison."

"This is spiritual warfare doctrine that most churches never teach, delivered by someone who's actually been in the fight."

"The distinction between biblical faith declaration and New Age manifestation is one of the most important clarifications I've encountered. Churches desperately need this."

"'Same demons, better packaging' isn't rhetoric—it's a thesis that the entire book proves chapter by chapter."

"The crisis chapter should be required reading for anyone in spiritual bondage—and for anyone trying to help them out of it."

"Most books on this topic either lack courage or lack compassion. This one has both—and that's rare."

"The Spiritual Deception Dictionary alone is worth the book. Finally, a field guide that calls things what they actually are."

"The bicycle tire analogy for the narrow road is one of the clearest illustrations of Matthew 7:14 I've ever read."

"This book asks the question most are afraid to ask: What if everything you thought was spiritual growth was actually spiritual bondage?"

"The Quick Reference chapter is genius—an emergency protocol for spiritual crisis that anyone can follow."

"The treatment of church infiltration isn't accusation—it's documentation. The examples are specific, current, and undeniable."

"What makes this different from other discernment books is the explanation of WHY deception works—not just that it exists."

"The chapter on helping others avoids the two extremes: condemning the deceived or coddling the deception. It threads the needle perfectly."

"The deliverance warning about demons returning eightfold is the most important caution in the book—and the most neglected truth in modern ministry."

"This isn't a book that tells you what to think. It's a book that teaches you how to see."

"The final line of the book—'Whose side are you on?'—isn't a threat. It's the only question that matters."

CHAPTER ONE

The Masking   The Un-Masking

LISTEN TO A SURVIVOR

B EFORE WE BEGIN, I'D like to introduce you to Morgane Rose, a survivor of Woo. She will tell you how she was drawn by traumas, anxieties, depressions, and fears in her life from childhood through an adult, along with spiritual experiences which drove her into Woo's deceptive hands. While her story might not be the same for each, many have experienced their own version of these same things. This is her story, in her words.

From Woo to Jesus

The enemy is very clever... NOT to compliment him... But clever in an evil way, obviously.

He has arranged to infiltrate the Church as an Institution and to create a getaway for people who sense something's not quite right with Religion. That way, the enemy is sure to harvest souls who are not educated about Jesus.

In everything that follows, in everything I'm sharing, by no means am I judging anyone. I've walked in dark alleys, I've repented (oh boy have I cried) so even if I might sound humorous or like I'm criticizing my past self, I'm not, I'm just honestly and boldly stating facts without judging anyone as a human.

So... yes... Religion never sat right with me. I can't remember how old I was, but from a young age, I was interested in mysterious and paranormal things. There was this show in the 90s called "Mystères" (a TV show where people would come and talk about some weird shizzle happening in their house or in their life—think "unexplained blood on the walls" and things like that). I'd be scared and also slightly frustrated because they'd always expose facts but never give an explanation. There would also be healers and psychics, and secretly, as a little girl, I wished I had the ability to help people and bring them relief by passing messages on to them from deceased loved ones and healing their physical pains.

Then came the age of catechism. In France, it's common for children to learn catechism. My parents aren't religious, although they had no choice but to go to Catholic school and follow catechism. I felt forced to go. I asked my parents if I could not go anymore, because I was not feeling good about it.

We didn't learn about Jesus per se, but all I remember is that we never studied the Bible. I never resonated with the Catholic Church for reasons I can't explain with words. Something never sat right with me in my young child's spirit. And not that long ago, I asked my parents if they ever studied the Bible at school or during catechism and their answer was a straight "No" (I know, shocking, right? That's how well the enemy has been working).

Anyway... So I made the terrible mistake from a young age of associating Jesus with Religion and I walked away from both, confused.

Life went on. I've always felt there was something else, something bigger. I would talk to God, even if I knew nothing about Him. I prayed as a child. I was a loner—an only child. I did have schoolmates, but outside of school, I had my dog and a couple of chickens, who were great friends. Also, I had two more that would never ever leave me: fear and anxiety.

But I wasn't aware it wasn't normal to feel that way. Long story short, I was a shy, traumatised introvert who was craving for love.

And the enemy knew that; he had already started working on me... from childhood, actually. I learned how to use a pendulum from a young age from my grandma, who had taught my Mom. I'd been so accurate from a young age.

I never questioned it because it was from my grandma. And we all have the image of a benevolent grandma. So yeah... there's that too... Generational "gifts" (aka curses, in that sense, are a real thing and often where it all starts subconsciously at least! Then add fear, anxiety and trauma to the mix...).

I know you might be wondering where I'm going with this, but I'm just setting up the scene so you see how sneaky the enemy is and how he starts to infiltrate from a young age, when you're innocent and just traumatised.

My uncle had healing abilities. He had a teacher—let's call him a guru who was said to be really good and his healing was very strong. I heard crazy stories, and I secretly admired that.

But one day he lost it and started taking his whole apartment apart. My aunt called home for help. Long story short, he had to go to a mental hospital and was never the same again. We hadn't added 2+2 at the time, but that's how the dark side operates. Nothing is ever free with the enemy.

I felt like my life was being guided by my dead grandfather, whom I gave credit as my spirit guide.

Life went on. I had a number of pen pals whom I cherished. Years later, I met a new pen friend, a Native American girl (A for future reference) with whom we connected. She was the first person ever to accept me as I was. We called ourselves soul sisters. She introduced me to her god (that I had the "brilliant" idea to get tattooed on my foot). I was ignorant, and I thought her god was the name of God.

She later introduced me to her Medicine Man (L for future reference), a wise man with a lot of occult knowledge that I genuinely thought was divine. Because the devil can't heal and doesn't mean well, right? Or so I thought...

One night, I had a vision of a man's right eye. I had never had a vision before, but I "intuitively" knew it was a vision. Of course I told A as soon as I woke up. Her answer was, "Oh it's probably L; he opened your 3rd eye. I told him you secretly wished as a child to have these abilities." A then said she'd ask L to send me a picture of himself so I could see if that eye was indeed his. L accepted, and I received the picture. I freaked out, because it was indeed his eye that I had seen in a vision that night... without ever seeing him in real life.

I started to face situations where wild animals would come my way, injured, and I'd pick them up, put my hands on them and they'd walk away. One day a little bird knocked itself on the window. I picked it up, put my hands on it and it recovered and flew away, then flew back around me and left. Of course, I was honored and felt special.

I got a message from L saying he and the Wakans were happy that I understood my gift was for the humans and also for the animals. I was speechless and overwhelmed with about a hundred questions I couldn't get answers to.

One night, I prayed to their god in my head as I was going to sleep. I didn't tell anyone I was praying, nor what I was praying about. I was basically talking to their god, saying whatever he wanted me to do, I accepted...

The next day, I got a message from L (remember; I didn't say anything to anyone about that prayer), saying how happy he was that I accepted my assignment. He knew exactly what I had been praying about. And to this day, this thought is not ok with me. It's like my mind was violated. But of course, at the time, I thought it was a validation that I was on the right path.

All I was craving was to be loved, to do things right and to be accepted. So, being "special" was part of that. I never had any ill intentions; it's important for me to insist on that. I was never into casting spells to manipulate anything in my favor. That is in no way an excuse; this is pure ignorance, and I was operating from wounds and traumas. But just to share that as an explanation of what my state of mind was at the time and how the enemy operates. Even when you don't have any intention of going down the dark path, he still finds a way. (But God always had my back in the background—which made me cry tears of gratitude when I realized how I gave credit to other things, people, dead people instead of Him, the Living God who sacrificed His Only Begotten Son for our sins, to save us!)

A few years went by, and things started going downwards. Moral harassment at work, even though I got promoted and had a very good status and salary as an executive. Things continued to spiral downward as work became a place I experienced visions, paranormal accidents and hauntings.

Later, my coworker, with whom I was getting along so well, started drinking and being violent to the staff, and to me. He almost hit me one day and screamed at me, towering over me. I thought he was going to destroy me that day.

I lost my Native American friends. L died, A got very sick (at least, so I was told) and it was radio silence almost overnight after years of back-and-forth emailing almost all day long. I felt lonely. I was lost.

One Saturday afternoon, I saw a sign at the Casino for a Wellness and Psychic Fair. Because of my background and the struggles I was facing at work, I saw it as a sign (which it was... but not from our Heavenly Father, obviously).

I walked in and sat with a psychic healer. He told me things that amazed me, like: how could he know I had had an ankle issue as a child? Fascinating, right? I'm being sarcastic, because this is exactly how the dark side operates: gaining your trust with insignificant details there's no way a stranger could have guessed.

He basically told me everything was going to be ok. When the session ended, I walked away unsure if I should feel reassured. He basically said a lot, but everything was void, nonsense and total foolishness.

I lost my job because the shareholders went bankrupt.

So, what did I do? I called the psychic I had seen about 1.5 years before. He said I could come to his office. I was scared... Scared of what he'd know about me, wondering if I'd have shocking news. I wasn't excited—in a way that felt heavy.

I sat there and, like the first time, he pulled cards, went silent and I was nervous. He said I'd find a job, and I'd be happy. He also said that A cast a spell on me, but he broke it and gave me a "magnetized cotton" that I needed to place under my pillow for a few days. I was scared that whatever spell was placed on me would come back, so I did what he told me. (Yuck! Honestly...).

I still remember having the same feeling as the first time—being amazed, yet unsettled. But he had said I'd find a job and all would be ok, so I shook that feeling and decided to choose it was going to be ok.

Now that I'm thinking back, it's almost like a part of me wasn't impressed and felt unfulfilled, with some "what now?" kind of vibe. This is exactly how the enemy gets people hooked... Always wanting to know more, because the pieces of info are true enough to make you believe it's real divine guidance, but never complete enough to give you satisfaction. That's how addictions start for some people. And I feel for them.

Knowing Jesus now, I can tell it's the total opposite. God will never get you "hooked" like that, and when the Holy Spirit gives you a message, it feels fulfilling, it feels special... it IS TRUTH. It never leaves you unsettled or confused.

A job offer fell from the sky, but something felt wrong. The interview went well, and any normal person would have been happy. I was confused and felt sick. Something was trying to tell me, "DO NOT GET THIS JOB."

My "healing gifts" had disappeared, everything had changed, and I was kind of depressed. Left with a newly gained awareness of the metaphysical but no one to answer my questions. I was lost.

But I knew it was actually God telling me not to take that job (even though the psychic had said I'd find a job and be happy...). I was unsettled and the day I declined; immediately a weight was lifted off my shoulders. And God told me I'd open my own business.

I decided to become a personal development coach and a Reiki master (yeah; I know... I have the "best" ideas sometimes—by now you're getting used to my sarcasm). A personal development coach because my rational mind told me anything spiritual could scare people.

As for Reiki master... My "logic" was that "I can't count on my own gifts because they let me down and disappeared, so I'll learn a system that can't let me down". Cue the spiral.

I got initiated. But once you're in there, the enemy loves to tease you with another level, then another type of Reiki, and another, and then crystals, and meditation, and then another Master came my way.

He forced me to talk about some trauma, saying that if I wouldn't tell him, I'd never heal. "Bro, be honest, you're just nosy and want to know" is really what I should have said. But I was so devastated as I was re-experiencing heavy trauma that I was in tears and felt forced to tell him... Which created another shock on top of the shock.

He then told me I wasn't initiated into Reiki "correctly" and I should go through it again, but with him, this time. (Of course, bro wanted that money.) But in a lucid moment, I saw his sneakiness (especially after he kind of blamed me for the trauma, saying it was actually my fault). So I ran away from him and never looked back. (Thanks to those two brain cells that decided to work that day in spite of the shock).

I can't really remember what was happening, but I remember I'd sometimes see "people" or "faces" (weird faces) looking down at me when I'd fall asleep or wake up—that "in-between" state. And it'd irritate me to the point of anger sometimes because I wouldn't understand why they'd be there and who the heck they were.

But my journey didn't stop here. I got into divination.

I discovered a YouTube Channel from a spiritual teacher, and we ended up becoming friends. One day she made a video about Twin Flames (if you don't know what that is, you're blessed—it's basically a New Age term that says someone else has the other half of your soul and it's a whole set of teachings designed to make you feel special and tolerate abuse, nothing more, nothing less. And it's dangerous).

Not long after that, I ended up at a summer market and heard the sound of a flute. It reminded me of my Native American friends, so I walked closer. This Native-American looking gentleman was playing, and I knew him... Or I felt and thought so. I had had a vision of him before. But I didn't know him in real life. I stood there in shock, and tears started rolling down my cheeks.

My friend said, "oh he must be your twin flame". One sentence that created almost as much harm as all the insults from the bullying I had experienced as a child. Because it made me spiral.

He and I became friends and went on a few dates. He had very narcissistic tendencies, and I fell for it. That caused so much pain and trouble in my life.

I was depressed and had a lot of anxiety. Following numbers and synchronicities. It was pretty ugly. Eventually, I let this man down after speaking my mind to him and never spoke to him again.

That YouTube friend later became delusional. She'd tell me how she's having conversations telepathically with her twin flame; like he'd bring her one million dollars so she could open her spiritual school. But she had clearly lost touch with reality. Eventually, she went to prison and became homeless.

I was in shock and realized how dangerous this whole Twin Flame thing was. New Age is full of wounded people preying on wounded people who are trying to heal and have a better life (as I was). Some of them aren't aware of what they're doing; yet others are.

God, in His infinite Glory and Mercy has always made sure I was kept safe, even if I have known some really dark and confusing times. He has always kept me physically safe and somehow mentally sane (aside from the depression, anxiety and eating disorder I forgot to mention, but there you go).

I got several certifications and then I developed my own (cringe warning) "energy healing and cleansing" technique. I'd cleanse people's energy, their trauma, their etheric parasites and even remove entities, break contracts and receive messages from their higher self. Yeah, I know I did cringe-warn. In just typing this, I feel like I need to wash my hands. But at the same time, I see the Glory of God.

Some sessions with clients were pretty intense. We started seeing aliens. I had also seen UFOs in real life.

I had weird sensations of being watched, remote-viewed; sometimes weird helicopters would fly above the house when I'd go in a session. It was a whole thing. Very dark...

In between, I met a man who became my partner. I won't go into much detail here because he is a famous artist, so I'll respect his privacy.

And if I'm honest, God was telling me to flee from Europe. Some force that was stronger than myself told me to leave against all odds, for every reason you can imagine. Love being the main one. So I left, terrified, scared, anxious, you name it... but I left.

My First Encounter with Jesus

He's a rasta and believes in Jesus. That's all I'll say about him. We're still friends today, even though we have parted ways. One day we were talking, and he showed me a Bible. I held one for the first time. I felt weird (because, remember; I had that religious thing that had never felt right from a young age). But I suddenly felt tears come up, and I couldn't hold them back. I remember telling him I'm sorry; I don't know what's happening. All I remember was that those tears felt warm, like homecoming. But I didn't understand. All I knew was that I was shaken and confused about why I cried so deeply and so uncontrollably, in a beautiful and loving way.

He tried to tell me how dangerous Reiki was, and when I told him about my Native American friends A and L, he asked me if I ever questioned the whole thing and if I trusted them. I said, "no, I had no reason to" but something upset me. I wanted to be upset with him for asking, but I also understood it might have seemed weird. But still, it didn't hit me.

I was defending my points (like a brainwashed person who genuinely believes a lie she calls "her truth").

Life happened. I had to go back to France for many reasons. I came home in shock; hiding it and pretending like it was the most rational thing to do. As I dove into work, I had another brilliant idea... take another training to increase my knowledge and abilities.

I won't mention the teacher's name because this person is renowned. But all I'll say is that this person was making fun of those he had taken as targets and would also have pet students. Spiritual gaslighting and narcissistic behavior.

Taking this training was one of my biggest mistakes ever. This person psychically attacked me after I unsubscribed and gave my honest reason why. That same night, I woke up dizzy with horrible nausea. The whole room was spinning; there was a dark, eerie vibe in my room. Something was clearly happening. I knew what and who it was from. So, I used my techniques, and it finally stopped.

Except that it didn't stop because I used "my so-called techniques". It stopped because God helped me even if I was an ignorant New Age practitioner who had given in to the cult of the ego without realizing it.

It's funny how when you step in dog poop and you smell something, you look around wondering what's happening, thinking someone else did... Because if it were you, you'd have noticed it, right? Well, being in the New Age is the same. You look at other people who do witchcraft and dark things, thinking you're not like them because you don't mean any harm, but you don't realize you have both feet in poop...

Fast forward to January 2022. I enrolled in a business-coaching program. I was doing market research and posted about it in a group for entrepreneurs. One name stood out to me: Rozella. I didn't know why, but I had a good feeling about this. We met on Zoom and had a good conversation. We became friends.

There was something about her—some sort of peaceful vibe and confidence. But not a confidence that comes from self, nothing like I had seen in the New Age. A form of confidence that felt Divine, beyond this world. A kind of confidence that's gentle, not arrogant, very humble. She said she was Christian. I remember thinking to myself; I don't know what that vibe is, but if that's what being a Christian brings, I want it.

She has never pushed her beliefs on me; she has never tried to convince me. She was just being herself, talking about her experience, her belief in our Lord and her Faith. That's when I discovered what true Faith looks like. And where her confidence was coming from: The Holy Spirit. The Trust that God has her back no matter what. So yeah... it wasn't confidence, as my mind had labeled it. It was FAITH, true Faith.

I started listening to Bible-study podcasts. I bought my first Bible and started reading it. But it was hard (mind you, I chose the KJV in Old English... I later bought the NKJV which is easier to understand). I fell off and eventually paused, but I'd still listen to Bible studies and started wearing the Cross as a pendent, because I genuinely felt like it (not in an unhealthy way, just because it was making me happy to show Jesus that I was trying my best).

I still had my New Age business... but started looking into Copywriting and Messaging. In parallel with that, all these years, God had been making sure I was developing other abilities than those foolish ones: I have always known how to optimize websites. My former self would say, "I intuitively knew", but I now know it was God giving me the knowledge.

I also started looking into testimonials from the New Age to Jesus, and one stood out to me from a lady named Jessica, who went from having a New Age business to being a Faith-Based Business coach. I also took a closer look at Doreen Virtue (whose decks of cards I had bought) who was also saved from the New Age by our Lord Jesus Christ, after being a famous author in this field.

God also led me to a YouTube Channel with Deliverance Prayers (by Noah Hines). I started listening and experienced huge realizations that were disturbing... How did I fall into that? How did that happen?

Something didn't feel right about my business but I was still serving my clients because I was figuring things out, trying to see what the limit was (if there was any, but now I know there isn't any limit, because the limit is simply not to do it at all anymore). I had my best consecutive months, but in June 2024, I felt God was starting to convict me and I was feeling horrible.

All these years, I thought I was serving God with a capital G. But I wasn't. I learned I had been wrong all my life, and it hurt to think I had misled others through my business.

I followed God's command and drew the line. June was the last month that I did this New Age business. I repented, I cried... But not to feel sorry for myself. I cried because how could God still want to save me after I'd rejected His only Begotten Son from a young age when I rejected religion?

How could He have Mercy that's so big and forgive me for my pure ignorance, pride and all these sins?

How could He forgive me for giving credit to my dead grandpa for finding me a job while it was Him all along?

My whole life has been guided not by dead ancestors, not by my Native American so-called friends, not by my teachers... but by God and God only.

This is really what made me cry.

He was the one who kept me safe even when I was abused. He was the one who made sure I'd never go too far and lose my marbles when I was in dark times that were psychologically dangerous. (I could've become paranoid; the feeling of being persecuted was real, after all, it was running in my bloodline, from my great-grandma's mental illness and suicide to my uncle becoming delusional and ending his days with a mental health condition no doctor ever managed to diagnose.)

But God made sure this wouldn't repeat, even if I had suicidal thoughts in the past. That's what the enemy will do; he'll trap you (or make you feel and think you're trapped) and tease you about the idea that ending your days is the sweetest option. But I never did.

Between July 2024 and now (early January 2026) God has delivered me.

I experienced the Python spirit coming out as well as other entities. I'm aware some say deliverance is not necessary, but when you dabble in the occult and God leads you there, it is. And trust me, I'm a whole different human now.

I got to meet Rozella, my first Christian friend, in person in September 2024 when she visited France—a few hours I'll never forget. I made new Christian friends and I now have weekly Bible Study Zoom Calls with my sister in Christ Elizabeth. I've cleaned up my life and removed some people who didn't have my highest good at heart, following God's instructions.

You only hear testimonies from the New Age to Jesus, never the other way around. There's a reason for it. Jesus is the Beginning and the End. Or actually the End of Earthly life and the Beginning of a New Life in Christ. He gave His life for us. That's how worthy God thinks we are, even when we do all sorts of foolishness.

This is also why I wanted to share my testimony as a way of giving back and of course saying to God how grateful I am and to help others who are in the shoes I once used to wear. Confused and lost as your whole belief system is collapsing and everything you thought was true was actually a lie.

The Danger of the Wellness Industry

In the Wellness Industry, you get to hear things like empowerment, self-love, taking your power back. At first, it sounds good and comes from good intentions. We have a saying in French "l'enfer est pavé de bonnes intentions" which would translate into something like, "the roads of hell are paved with good intentions". It's an explanation but never an excuse.

Then you get to hear about "your thoughts create your reality" (while it's really God who's THE Supreme Creator). You're told you get to co-create, you're responsible for your own misery and if you keep attracting unpleasant situations, it's because you have blocks and subconscious beliefs. Basically, you're being told you're messing up and if you want to have a better life, you need to align your thoughts with the reality you want and "fake it 'til you make it" (hello delulu, you're not the solulu!).

Then you're led to fall into manifestation and the Law of Attraction.

The New Age is the kingdom of ego, a guilt-trip festival where you're shamed for talking about the negative. They're telling you to ignore your problems because otherwise you'll attract more of them.

Basically, if you have a bad life, it's your fault; you're doing something wrong. And if nothing's working, then you're doing something wrong because "it works for me so it'll work for you if you do it right."

You start opening a can of worms, and then you meet people; you get tempted to try this and then that...

Why? Because nothing freaking works! If Reiki had worked, I wouldn't have tried another discipline. Subconsciously we know but we don't want to see it, because we seek safety, we seek healing, wellness, love, attention, whatever it is.

Only Jesus can provide it. When you truly meet Jesus, all those things go straight to the garbage. I threw crystals, decks of cards, books, destroyed all my notes and made sure to close all doors.

So yes, your New Age friends will tell you, you've changed. People won't understand. But it doesn't matter, all that matters is God and He will always tell you what to say (or not, because sometimes you think you need to say something but God knows it's a trap from the enemy and it's best to block the person).

The enemy creates confusion, teases, and makes you doubt.

I used to think if these things were evil, I'd feel it because it'd be ugly, dark and mean.

But because I rejected religion, I made the mistake of rejecting Jesus. By not knowing Jesus, I didn't know God's Word; therefore, I didn't know the enemy either. So I didn't know about the danger.

Now I can clearly and loudly say Jesus is the only way.

CHAPTER TWO

The Masking   The Un-Masking

YOU MAY NOT AGREE WITH ME AND I DON'T CARE!

ACTUALLY, I DO CARE ABOUT YOU AS A PERSON. JUST NOT WHETHER YOU AGREE WITH ME.

H ERE'S THE DEAL: I'M going to tell you some things that'll probably tick you off.

Good.

If you're not uncomfortable, you're not growing.

THERE'S ONLY ONE TRUE GOD

Let's get this straight right from the start. The God of Israel—Yahweh—Papa God; is the ONLY True and Living God. Period. End of discussion.

THIS I WILL PROVE

"But Tom, there are many gods, many paths, many—"

Stop right there.

Yes, there are many spiritual beings and gods in this world. Many powers. Many voices screaming for your attention. But there's ONLY ONE who spoke the universe into existence, holds it together by the word of His mouth, is God over ALL, and deserves your worship.

The rest?

Pretenders.

Liars.

Spiritual CON artists.

Don't like that? Think I'm being narrow-minded?

Good.

Keep reading anyway.

I'M NOT HERE TO MAKE

FRIENDS

After fifty-five years of walking with Papa God. Terminal cancer miraculously healed—a football-sized tumor melted in 24 hours while I was riding home on my motorcycle. Seeing storms dissipated instantly. Seeing demons stopped. Watching angels working. ALL real stuff. Not churchianity or religious fairy tales.

I'm not some seminary graduate who learned about God from books. I'm not some denominational puppet regurgitating religious talking points. And I'm definitely not some "spiritual but not religious" person dabbling in cosmic nonsense.

I'm someone who's LIVED this. Who's walked through the fire and came out knowing the difference between God's voice and everything else trying to get in your head. I've experienced His unquestionable and incomparable Presence and Power through these many years. Read my first two books, *THE DAILY STAND* and *SET THE CAPTIVES FREE*.

THERE ARE ONLY TWO SOURCES OF SPIRITUAL POWER IN THE UNIVERSE

Two. Period. Not ten. Not "many paths up the same mountain." Two.

God's Kingdom or Satan's kingdom. Light or darkness. Truth or deception.

By now you've probably already put me in a box so you can dismiss everything I'm about to tell you, calling me: "Religious fanatic." "Fundamentalist." "Narrow-minded."

FINE.

STAY IN YOUR BOX IF IT MAKES YOU FEEL SAFE.

But here's what I know: The people who scream loudest about being "open-minded" are usually the ones trapped in the biggest boxes of all. They just decorated their prisons to look like palaces.

YOU THINK YOU CAN'T BE DECEIVED?

Right now, you might be thinking:

"I'm a solid Christian. I know my Bible. And I know I can't be fooled or deceived."

Or: "I'm a religious person, and my denomination will keep me safe."

Or: "I'm not stuck in anybody's interpretation of religion, because I know better."

Or: "I'm too smart for this. I've studied comparative religion, psychology, quantum physics. I'm beyond your simple-minded theology."

Or: "I'm spiritual, not religious. I've transcended your limited understanding. I'm just too smart for you and your book. I'm in tune with the vast spiritual realm, not limited by your narrow interpretations. I have so much more wisdom and experience you just can't understand."

ALL concluding...

"So, this book will most likely be a waste of my valuable

time."

HERE'S THE MILLION-DOLLAR QUESTION:

Are you willing to find out if you're wrong?

Because, by the end of this book, you're going to discover something that'll shake you to your core:

The people who think they can't be deceived are usually the most deceived of all.

The religious ones think their denomination protects them. The intellectual ones think their education protects them. The spiritual ones think their experiences protect them.

They're ALL wrong.

THE REAL QUESTION

So here it is, the only question that matters:

Are you free of deception?

Not, "Do you think you are?"

ARE YOU?

Because if you're not, everything else you believe—your theology, your spiritual practices, your entire worldview—could be built on lies.

And that should scare the hell out of you.

LITERALLY.

CHAPTER THREE

WHY PART TOO? WHAT'S THE DIFFERENCE?

Part One of SET THE CAPTIVES FREE

W<small>AS ABOUT CHURCH CAPTIVITY.</small> Religious systems. Denominational prisons. False Belief Systems that have infected nearly every church, religion, and denomination on the planet. For believers who need freedom from captivity, not only in the churches, but for those who've left the churches because of abuse.

In other words, I told you how your own church might be keeping you in spiritual chains.

Fun stuff, right?

Part "TOO" is about EVERYTHING ELSE TRYING TO DESTROY YOUR SOUL

All the spiritual garbage infecting the world AND the church. New Age nonsense. Energy healing. Manifestation madness. Ancient wisdom lies. The whole buffet of demonic deception that people are gorging themselves on—thinking it's spiritual food. Addressing all the "gods" of this world.

Apparently, the enemy wasn't satisfied with just corrupting church doctrine. He had to go full-court press on everything spiritual.

If you thought church captivity was bad, wait until you see what's been creeping into your sanctuary while you weren't paying attention.

THE CHURCH IS INFECTED

If you're a Bible-believing Christian, you probably think you can spot worldly deception from outer space. You've got your spiritual radar up watching out for the obvious stuff—witchcraft, psychics, fortune telling.

You're like, "Not me! I see you coming a mile away with your crystal balls and tarot cards."

But what about the stuff that's already sitting IN your church pew?

Christian yoga classes in the fellowship hall. Enneagram workshops for spiritual growth. Contemplative prayer retreats. Lectio Divina meditation. Centering prayer circles. Breathwork "ministry." Energy healing "ministry." Manifestation theology. All dressed up in "Jesus language."

False spiritual Woo has infiltrated the churches.

YOU MIGHT BE SHOCKED!

While you might not be shocked that the world has been taken captive under the god and gods of this world's deceptions—you might be shocked at how many good, sincere believers are practicing this stuff. Defending it as the Gospel truth. Getting offended when you dare to question their "deeper spirituality."

Many sincere believers are caught up in many false and unholy mixtures. They've been taken captive, and they're completely clueless about it.

Yet for all captives alike, Jesus proclaimed,

"I've come to set the captives free."

I'M NOT AN EXPERT ON LIVING THE DECEPTION

Here's what I WON'T do: Pretend I've personally walked through every false spiritual path out there. I haven't been a witch, a New Ager, a Buddhist, or a crystal healer. Sorry to disappoint those of you who are only looking for juicy "I used to channel demons but now I'm saved" testimonies.

That's not my story.

Instead, I've been walking with Papa God and dealing with these demons from a spiritual warfare perspective for over fifty-five years.

I've watched people be set free from this stuff. I've seen the spiritual warfare behind it. I know what Papa God's Word says about it. And I've watched people get delivered from it over and over again.

That's my qualification: Five decades of watching God set captives free.

There are many others who have direct experience with them, as you heard in Chapter One. Including others who've authored valuable books, talk on podcasts, and teach about the deceptions they were under. If you want someone who's "been there, done that," go find them. There are plenty of them, and many are excellent.

The only valuable perspectives I can bring to you here are:

The revealing of the hidden secrets behind the god and gods of this world.

The unveiling of the Truth from the Word of God.

How to be set free.

And most importantly, "**Papa's heart**" and perspective for those caught in deception. Which is LOVE and redemption versus condemnation as others might do.

This book is for people who want to know how to recognize deception and get FREE from it.

LET'S ESTABLISH THE TRUTH ONCE AND FOR ALL

Before we dive into all the false gods and spiritual counterfeits, let's get one thing crystal clear:

GOD IS GOD. PERIOD. DEAL WITH IT.

He's the One and Only, True God

There is NO other True God

Everything else?

False gods.

There may be many "gods" in this world. Demon rulers under Satan, the *god of this world,* masquerading as enlightened beings. Spiritual CON artists with fancy names and empty promises.

But none of them is God.

"But Tom, that's so narrow-minded. What about all the spiritual paths? All the wisdom traditions? The universe is so much bigger than your little box!"

Oh, my box? Let me tell you about my "little" box.

SCIENCE PROVES GOD IS GOD

God is the One who spoke the world into existence in six sentences over six days. Not millions of years. Not evolution. Six literal days.

Think I'm scientifically ignorant? Think I'm some backwoods fundamentalist who's never heard of physics? Think again.

I have several engineering degrees centered on math and science. Including Electrical Engineering, Computer Science, Information Technologies, and more. I've not only worked for top companies in these fields, but successfully ran my own Hardware, Software and System Design Company for over forty-five years.

Now let me blow your mind with some atomic physics that every scientist knows but can't explain:

If you read **THE DAILY STAND**, you'd know I explained scientifically, by the atomic structure that's inside of *everything*, that God not only spoke the world into being, but that He still holds everything together by the Word of His mouth.

For those who haven't read my first book, let me quote a section from Chapter Seven, "God Can Do Anything", to prove to you why God is God and science proves it. Along with revealing what the real truth is behind the "big band theory."

Even if you've read it, it's worth seeing again.

As quoted from THE DAILY STAND

GOD CREATED ALL BY THE WORD OF HIS MOUTH

"In the beginning God created the heavens and the earth. The earth was formless and void, and darkness was over the surface of the deep, and the Spirit of God was moving over the surface of the waters.

Then God said, 'Let there be light';

And, there was light...

Then God said, 'Let there be an expanse in the midst of the waters, and let it separate the waters from the waters.';

And, it was so...

Then God said, 'Let the waters below the heavens be gathered into one place, and let the dry land appear';

And, it was so...

Then God said, 'Let the earth sprout vegetation: plants yielding seed, and fruit trees on the earth bearing fruit after their kind with seed in them';

And, it was so...

Then God said, 'Let there be lights in the expanse of the heavens to separate the day from the night, and let them be for signs and for seasons and for days and years; and let them be for lights in the expanse of the heavens to give light on the earth';

And, it was so...

Then God said, 'Let the waters teem with swarms of living creatures, and let birds fly above the earth in the open expanse of the heavens.'...

Then God said, 'Let the earth bring forth living creatures after their kind: cattle and creeping things and beasts of the earth after their kind';

And, it was so...

Then God said, 'Let Us make man in Our image, according to Our likeness'...

And, it was so." (Genesis 1:1–31)

GOD SAID IT, AND IT WAS SO

GOD HOLDS ALL THINGS TOGETHER BY THE WORD OF HIS MOUTH

Psalm 33:6 tells us,

"By THE WORD of the LORD the heavens were made, and by THE BREATH of HIS MOUTH ALL their host."

And in Hebrews 1:3, we're told,

"The Son is the radiance of God's glory and the exact representation of His nature and being, sustaining and upholding ALL THINGS by THE WORD of HIS [MOUTH] POWER."

Power in the Greek is 'dunamis' (do-na-miss), meaning "power," "might," "strength—ability," "miracles," "miraculous powers."

ATOMS AND THEIR PARTICLES

Let's take a tangent and review some basic facts about atoms, and then I'll explain why.

Protons, electrons, and neutrons are the atomic particles that make up the atom.

Atoms are microscopically tiny, but the atomic particles inside the atom are much smaller than that—so small, in fact, that science has determined that atoms are mostly composed of open space.

Protons have positive nuclear and magnetic power. All of them reside together in the center (nucleus) of the atom along with all the neutrons.

Neutrons are neutral. They have no nuclear or magnetic power. Some scientists theorize that neutrons insulate protons, but that theory is unsubstantiated and easily challenged.

Electrons have negative nuclear and magnetic power, all flying in orbit around the nucleus. Atoms usually have an equal number of protons and electrons or, in the case when one electron has been added or removed, it's called an ion.

Electrons travel at the speed of light. Their size and distance are proportional to the planets orbiting the sun.

That's a lot of open space.

The sun has an incredible magnetic force—so great, in fact, that it holds all the rotating planets in orbit.

In the same way, the magnetic power of the positive protons in the nucleus is equally great—so substantial that it can hold **ALL** the electrons in orbit.

This takes a tremendous amount of power in and of itself, but it takes even much more power when the electrons are traveling in orbit at the speed of light.

MAGNETIC FORCE

We're getting to the point, but for a moment, let's take another tangent—oh no, it's a double tangent! How will we be able to get back?

So let's talk about magnetic force with the analogy of two magnets.

The first basic part of magnetic law—opposite forces attract.

The positive side of one magnet will immediately attract the negative side of a second magnet.

Example: If you hold two magnets near each other, with one's positive side near the other's negative side, they will immediately "snap" together.

The second basic part of magnetic law—like forces repel (push apart).

The positive side of one magnet will immediately push away from the positive side of a second magnet. As well as the reverse is true. The negative side of one magnet will immediately push away from the negative side of a second magnet.

Example: If you hold two magnets near each other, positive to positive or negative to negative, they will immediately "jump" or "fly" apart from each other.

SO BACK TO ATOMS

The magnetic force of protons, all huddled together in the nucleus, is so powerful that it holds all electrons in orbit—electrons flying at the speed of light and proportionally at the distance of the planets from the sun.

That type of magnetic force is monumental—massive, enormous, immense, and overwhelmingly powerful.

So, the big question: If protons are ALL POSITIVELY CHARGED, ALL HUDDLED TOGETHER in the NUCLEUS, then why don't the protons "blow" apart from each other?

By all scientific understanding of magnetic forces, they should!

What holds them together? Neutrons?

Nope.

No science validates that theory.

That's just not what they do. They just don't have enough insulating capability to do that, and because the atomic particles are so small, proportionally, having so much open space between them, that would never work.

Then what does hold them together?

Bottom line: Science just doesn't know.

Science cannot address or explain why.

So, they insert numerous theories about other tiny sub-particles made up of "baryons," "mesons," "leptons," "bosons," "gluons," "hadrons," "pions," "kaons" and others made up by "quarks" that might affect the atom. Pure guesswork. Not too scientific, guys. These other subatomic particles are so tiny in comparison to protons and neutrons that they have no effect. As well as most of these subatomic particles are not stable—lasting only microseconds.

SO, WHAT DOES?

The Word of God.

The Word of His Mouth as spoken by Him in Genesis.

You say, "WHAT?"

Yes, God holds everything together by the Word of His Mouth.

God defies (or goes beyond) science—because God made science.

WHAT IF GOD DIDN'T HOLD THEM TOGETHER?

If God didn't hold the atoms together, they'd blow apart as all magnetic science denotes they should.

Then what would happen? Every atom's proton's overwhelming positive magnetic force would cause them to repel, disperse, and fly far away from each other.

Therefore, with the nucleus dispersed, the electrons and neutrons would just float away—having nothing to hold them in place.

As the protons dispersed, each individual proton's positive magnetic force would attract one floating electron—that would then fly in orbit around that proton, creating a new atom.

What type of atom would you end up with when you have one proton and one electron? Hydrogen—hydrogen gas.

What does Genesis 1 say? "The earth was formless and void."

Many scientists theorize it may've been a bunch of hydrogen gas floating around before they say the "big bang theory" happened.

Hydrogen gas—again.

Getting the connection yet?

Do you want to know what the "big bang" really is?

THEN GOD SAID, "... LET THERE BE ...", AND IT WAS SO

And from the hydrogen gas was formed every kind of atom—that then formed everything else. Pretty amazing if you take the time to let that sink in!

What's more amazing is that it's STILL ALL HELD TOGETHER by the Word of His Mouth!

If not, we already know that EVERYTHING WOULD FLY APART and RETURN to HYDROGEN GAS.

So, for those of us who've ever wondered or doubted if God is really here, really cares, is really in charge, or can really do the things the Bible says He can do, then just stop and think.

If He did not hold you, me, everyone, and everything in this world together, we'd just be a bunch of gas—**and science proves it**.

as quoted from THE DAILY STAND

Now We've Established the Truth:

If God stopped speaking for one nanosecond, every atom in the universe would instantly fly apart into hydrogen gas. You, me, your coffee cup, the planet—everything would cease to exist faster than you could blink.

THAT's how powerful He is.

THAT's why He's the Only True God.

Are you still worried about whether He's powerful enough to handle your problems?

Your "spiritual guides" can't hold an atom together. Your "ascended masters" can't maintain nuclear force. Your "universal consciousness" can't prevent molecular collapse. They're not powerful enough.

Only GOD can do that.

And He does it every split second of every day.

When His Word / Bible / Scripture tells us why Creation is the Truth—as we just learned—then we need to understand when the same tells us **He's** the One and Only, True and Living God; He is.

SO WHAT DOES THAT MAKE EVERYTHING ELSE?

If there's only ONE True God who literally holds the universe together by His Word—and science proves this whether or not scientists admit it—what does that make all the other "gods" people are worshipping, channeling, and getting guidance from?

FALSE GODS.

COUNTERFEITS.

IMPOSTERS.

DEMONS, with better marketing.

And if you're messing around with them—even if you call it "Christian" or "spiritual growth" or "healing ministry"—you're playing with fire that will eventually burn you badly.

Time to figure out which side of this spiritual war you're actually on.

CHAPTER FOUR

WHO ARE THE FALSE GODS?

ANGELS OF LIGHT

H ERE'S SATAN'S MASTERPIECE STRATEGY: He doesn't show up with horns and a pitchfork. He shows up looking like an angel.

"Even Satan disguises himself as an angel of light. Therefore it is not surprising if **his servants also disguise themselves** as servants of righteousness." (2 Corinthians 11:14-15)

This isn't just theological theory. This is Satan's actual battle plan. Because apparently, the guy who's been lying since the Garden of Eden figured out that obvious evil gets rejected, but beautiful, spiritual-looking evil gets embraced with open arms.

Who knew the father of lies would be so good at marketing?

The most dangerous deceptions don't come with warning labels. They come with soft music, beautiful imagery, and promises of peace, love, and enlightenment. They quote Scripture. They use Christian terminology. They promise to make you more spiritual, more connected to God, more authentic than those "ordinary" believers.

And they're not just infiltrating your culture—they're infiltrating your church, your Bible study, your prayer group, and quite possibly, your own spiritual practices.

THE SAME OLD DEMONS WITH NEW BUSINESS CARDS

The "gods" people are channeling, praying to, and receiving "wisdom" from today aren't new spiritual beings. They're the same demonic entities that have been in the deception business since Day One.

They Just Got Tired of the Whole "Terrifying Ancient Deity" Routine and Hired a Better PR Team

In ancient times, they ruled through fear. People trembled before Zeus, bowed to Apollo, made blood sacrifices to Molech. They built massive temples, performed elaborate rituals, and lived in terror of these "gods." The deception was obvious—these were dark, demanding entities that required appeasement and lived off human terror.

But fear-based religion eventually gets old. People start questioning why their "gods" are so angry, demanding, and destructive. So, the devil and his demons changed tactics. They went to Spiritual Marketing 101 and learned that honey catches more flies than vinegar.

Nowadays, they have better marketing, that we buy "hook, line and sinker."

Today, these same demonic entities present themselves as loving guides, enlightened masters, and benevolent angels. Zeus became "The Universe." Apollo became "Your Higher Self." Isis became "Divine Feminine Energy." Molech became "The God Within."

Same demons.

Same agenda.

Better packaging.

Instead of demanding blood sacrifices, they demand your discernment.

Instead of requiring temple prostitution, they require spiritual compromise.

Instead of physical idols, they create mental idols—false concepts of God, truth, and spirituality that sound enlightened but lead straight to hell.

Here's the kicker: They've convinced millions of Christians that these "new" spiritual experiences are actually deeper, more authentic Christianity.

And because of the deep indoctrination and acceptance in the church, many have accepted this as the norm.

THE GREAT SPIRITUAL REBRANDING CAMPAIGN

Remember when Christians could spot occult practices from a mile away? Back when witchcraft was evil, séances were demonic, psychics were dangerous, and astrology belonged in the "avoid like the plague" category? When tarot cards were satanic, eastern meditation was pagan, crystal healing was witchcraft, and satanic and devil worship were not acceptable in any form?

Those were simpler times. The lines were clear. It was black and white. Good versus evil. God versus the devil. Light versus darkness.

Where people clearly defined these things as bad and wrong.

Then Satan launched the most successful rebranding campaign in history.

He took every occult practice that Christians used to reject and gave it a spiritual makeover. These days, it's all been updated, repainted, rebranded, and repackaged as the mainstream, widely accepted, "wide road" of Woo spirituality.

Witchcraft didn't disappear—it became "energy healing" and "manifestation." Same power source, same techniques, same demonic results. But now it's practiced in churches disguised under the banner of "healing ministry." Women who would never touch a Ouija board are now learning to "channel healing energy" and "manifest God's blessings."

It's the same occult power, just with "Jesus stickers" slapped on top. Because everything's better with a little religious branding, right?

Séances became "channeling," "spirit communication," and "angelic encounters." Instead of scary parlor rooms with crystal balls, you have beautiful conference centers with soft lighting where "Christian" mediums teach people to connect with "angels" and "spirit guides." The dead are still being contacted. Demons are still being invited. But now it's disguised under "prophetic ministry" or "angelic experiences."

Psychic readings transformed into "intuitive counseling," "spiritual direction," and "prophetic insights." Same demonic information source.

Same fortune-telling spirits. Just delivered in a church setting by someone with a ministry license instead of a neon sign.

The same people who used to go to palm readers and fortune tellers now pay "Christian" counselors to give them "prophetic insights" about their future. Same demonic information. Same source of knowledge. Just delivered in a church setting by someone with a ministry license.

Astrology became "cosmic consciousness," "reading the signs," and "divine timing." Christians who would never check their horoscope are now studying "biblical astronomy," looking for "signs in the heavens," and planning their lives around "God's cosmic calendar." They're still letting celestial bodies guide their decisions instead of God's Word—they just found Bible verses to justify it. Same demonic guidance system, different vocabulary.

Tarot cards evolved into "oracle cards" and "prophetic guidance tools." The pictures got prettier, the messages got more positive, the demonic source stayed exactly the same. But hey, since you can buy them in Christian bookstores now labeled under "prophetic" and "hearing God's voice," that makes them OK, right?

This isn't accidental. This is strategic warfare. Satan studied what Christians would reject and what they would accept. He learned our language, adopted our terminology, and figured out how to make occult practices look like deeper Christianity.

And it worked. Brilliantly.

It may not be that surprising that this rebranding became widely accepted in the world, but it should be surprising that it has become so widely accepted in the churches and among believers who should know better.

THE TROJAN HORSE

LIVING IN THE SANCTUARY

PERVERSION IN THE CHURCH

What we would have judged as garbage and thrown out of the church forty years ago, we now welcome with open arms and call it revival. Adopted in the churches under new guises. The enemy has successfully smuggled his deceptions past our spiritual security system by wrapping them in Christian terminology and delivering them through trusted spiritual leaders.

It's like spiritual identity theft, but here the victims are helping the thieves.

Take "Christian" yoga, for example. Pastors who would never allow Hindu priests to teach in their churches are now hosting yoga classes in their fellowship halls. They tell their congregations that they're just "borrowing the stretches" and "Christianizing" the practice. But you can't separate yoga postures from yoga spirituality any more than you can separate cocaine from its narcotic effects. Each pose is a form of worship to Hindu deities. Each breathing technique is designed to open your spirit to demonic influence.

Just because you can slap "Jesus stickers" on a bottle of poison, the contents are still deadly.

Contemplative prayer sounds so spiritual, so deep, so mature. Churches are teaching their members to empty their minds, repeat sacred words, and enter altered states of consciousness to "encounter God." This is Eastern meditation with a thin Christian veneer. The goal is the same: bypass your rational mind, suppress your discernment, and open yourself to whatever spiritual entity wants to communicate. When you empty your mind in the name of spirituality, you don't get more of God—you get whatever demon is waiting for an unguarded entrance.

The Enneagram has become the church's favorite personality tool. Christian leaders are using this Sufi mysticism system to understand themselves and counsel others. They don't know—or don't care—that it comes from Islamic occultism and is designed to connect people with demonic spiritual guides. They just know it gives them insights into human behavior, so they baptized it with Christian language and called it wisdom. Problem solved!

"Prophetic" art workshops are teaching Christians to paint and draw while in altered states, believing they're channeling images from God. Students are instructed to empty their minds, surrender control, and let "the Spirit" guide their hands. What they're actually doing is practicing automatic art—a classic occult technique where demons control human actions. The beautiful, spiritual-looking artwork becomes a doorway for demonic influence, and the "prophetic" messages become demonic communications disguised as God's voice.

Soaking prayer sessions are teaching people to lie still for hours, empty their minds, and wait for supernatural experiences. They're told this is how they encounter God's presence. But biblical prayer is active, conscious, and discerning. When you shut down your mind and passively wait for spiritual experiences, you're practicing the same technique used in séances, channeling sessions, and occult rituals.

While there is truth in Scripture about "waiting upon the Lord" and about "waiting in His presence to find Him", this is different. Without proper balanced teaching from the Word and understanding THE PEACE of God ruling and guarding your hearts and minds, these practices will be spiritually harmful. When you enact a human effort to empty your mind without that understanding, you will make yourself available to whatever spiritual entity wants to interact with you—and it's rarely the Holy Spirit.

Angel encounters are being promoted as normal Christian experiences. Which can be true, but not as the new false spiritualists are teaching. The Scripture does tell us we entertain angels unaware (Hebrews 13:2). There are true and valid experiences with the angels of God. But the rest are pure garbage. Learn a lot more where I describe the differences in **THE DAILY STAND** where there's a full chapter on Angels.

In the new false spirituality, people are being taught to seek direct communication with angels, receive guidance from them, and even worship alongside them. But the Bible warns us that Satan's demons masquerade as angels of light. When Christians start seeking angel encounters instead of staying focused on Jesus and His Word, they're opening themselves to demonic deception. Every "angel" that leads you away from Scripture, contradicts biblical truth, or makes you dependent on supernatural experiences is not from God. Funny how these "angels" always seem to lead people away from simple faith in God's Word and toward dependency on supernatural experiences.

"Holy" laughter manifestations are being promoted as evidence of God's joy and approval. People are rolling on floors, making animal noises, and losing control of their bodies, calling it the movement of the Holy Spirit. Unfortunately, this is kundalini energy—a demonic spiritual force that operates through the chakra system. When people surrender their self-control and allow their bodies to be taken over by spiritual forces, they're not experiencing God's joy—they're experiencing demonic possession disguised as religious ecstasy.

We call it revival. God calls it rebellion.

The same false gods that demanded worship in ancient temples are now receiving worship in modern sanctuaries. The only difference is the vocabulary, the venue, and the background music. The spiritual source, the demonic agenda, and the ultimate destination remain exactly the same.

FALSE PROPHETS WITH SEMINARY DEGREES

In **THE DAILY STAND** and **SET THE CAPTIVES FREE** I clearly define what are true versus false prophets. I will not quote all of it here. But for reference, here's a small part:

As quoted from THE DAILY STAND

What is a prophet?

The word **prophet** breaks down into two parts—"pro" which means "forth" and "phet" which means to "speak"—therefore, the word prophet means to "speak forth."

"Beloved, DO NOT BELIEVE EVERY SPIRIT, but TEST [analyze, examine] the SPIRITS to see whether they are FROM GOD, **because MANY FALSE PROPHETS have gone out into the world.**" (1 John 4:1)

Ezekiel 13:3–6 says,

"This is what the Sovereign Lord says: WOE to the FOOLISH PROPHETS who follow their own spirit and have SEEN NOTHING!

Their VISIONS are FALSE and their DIVINATIONS a LIE.

Even though the LORD has NOT SENT THEM, They SAY, 'THE LORD DECLARES,' and expect Him to fulfill their words."

So, what is a false prophet?

He or she is someone under the influence of a false Christ (a false anointing), a false god.

Make sense?

FALSE ANOINTINGS CREATE FALSE PROPHETS.

A prophet of God, under God's Anointing, speaks forth the CURRENT WORD of the Living God.

Conversely, a false prophet speaks forth the deceptions of false Christs, false gods, and false anointings.

So, don't fall prey or believe everything you hear.

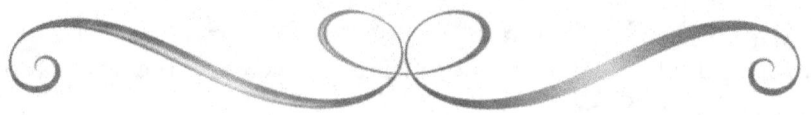

As quoted from THE DAILY STAND

Every false god needs a spokesperson.

Someone to legitimize their message. Someone to make their deception sound biblical. Someone to give them access to God's people.

In ancient times, false prophets were easier to spot. They served obviously pagan gods, promoted clearly unbiblical practices, and operated outside the community of God's people. Today's false prophets are much more sophisticated. They have seminary degrees, pastor large churches, write bestselling books, and speak at major Christian conferences. It's like having a wolf with a theology degree leading the sheep.

But their spiritual source is the same: They operate under false anointings.

A true prophet of God operates under God's anointing—the Spirit of Truth. He speaks God's current word for God's people. His messages align with Scripture. He produces fruit that draws people closer to Jesus, deeper love for God's Word, and clearer discernment between truth and deception.

A false prophet operates under a false anointing—a demonic spirit masquerading as God's Spirit. He speaks the enemy's current deception disguised as a greater or new revelation of God's word. His messages sound biblical but contradict the Scripture's clear meaning. His fruit produces confusion about God's Word, compromise with worldly spirituality, and dependency on supernatural experiences instead of faith in God's promises.

Here's What Makes Them So Dangerous:

They believe their own deceptions. They're not consciously trying to deceive people. They genuinely think they're hearing from God and serving His people. But they're operating under a false anointing, so everything they produce is spiritually contaminated, no matter how sincere their intentions.

How Do You Tell the Difference?

Jesus gave us the test: "You will know them by their fruits." (Matthew 7:16)

What fruit is their ministry producing in people's lives?

Are people becoming more dependent on God's Word or on supernatural experiences?

Are they developing stronger discernment or greater openness to spiritual confusion?

Are they focusing more on a personal relationship with Jesus or on spiritual phenomena?

A false prophet will always lead people away from the simplicity of faith in Christ and toward the complexity of spiritual experiences. They make God's people dependent on them instead of dependent on God's Word. They promote mixture instead of purity. They create spiritual hunger that can never be satisfied because they're feeding people spiritual junk food instead of the bread of life.

THE TWO-QUESTION ACID TEST

Here's your spiritual deception detector for any spiritual teaching, practice, prophet, or experience. It only takes two questions, but they'll save your spiritual life:

Question 1: Does it Align with God's Word?

Not just using biblical vocabulary—does it actually align with Scripture's clear meaning? [Always in the light of the original Greek and Hebrew, not being limited to any one translation.] Does it contradict any biblical principle? Does it require you to reinterpret or ignore parts of the Bible?

If it doesn't line up with God's Word, it's from a false god. Period.

No exceptions, no gray areas, no "but it feels so spiritual and right."

Question 2: Does it Produce God's PEACE?

"**THE PEACE** of God, **which Surpasses ALL Comprehension [Understanding]**, will guard your hearts and minds through Christ Jesus." (Philippians 4:7) God's True PEACE brings clarity, rest, and confidence in His Word. If a spiritual practice produces anxiety, confusion, spiritual hunger that can't be satisfied, or dependency on experiences instead of faith, it's not from God. [Learn the difference about **THE PEACE** of God, as taught in *THE DAILY STAND*.]

That's it. Two Questions.

Two Answers: THE WORD of God and HIS PEACE.

If any spiritual teaching, practice, or prophet fails either test, reject it immediately. Don't try to "redeem" it. Don't look for the good parts. Don't make excuses for the concerning elements.

Reject it completely and run in the opposite direction.

Run. Fast.

Because here's what's coming: The false gods are positioning themselves for the final spiritual battle of human history. They're not coming with obvious evil anymore—that strategy failed. They're coming as "angels of light," ministers of righteousness, and deeper spiritual experiences.

They're going to offer you spiritual experiences that feel amazing, teachings that sound enlightened, and practices that promise to make you more spiritual than you've ever been. With the hidden pride element, you're now part of the "greater revelation" of God's Word in these last days.

And if you don't know how to test the spirits, you're going to fall for it hook, line, and sinker.

It's time to get your discernment muscles in shape.

The battle is coming, and the "angels of light" are far more dangerous than demons in the dark.

CHAPTER FIVE

WOO

WHAT IS IT?

I N A FEW QUOTES from *The American Heritage® Dictionary of the English Language, 5th Edition,* **Woo** means:

1. To seek the affection of (someone, especially a woman) with the intent to marry or begin a romantic relationship.

2. To gain the favor of (someone) or move (someone) to do something by entreaties or inducements; i.e., "an ad campaign that wooed customers away from their usual brand."

3. To court solicitously; to invite with importunity.

In the normal world's definition, **Woo** means to seek the love, favor, or attention of someone, often through charming gestures. As well as referring to attempts to attract or persuade someone toward a particular interest or cause.

THE WOO DECEPTION

In the spiritual world, **Woo** uses love, favor, charming gestures, or enticements in the attempt to attract or persuade someone into a particular spiritual interest or cause. On the surface, it looks good. Yet underneath it, there's something very sinister. The rebranding and repackaging of ancient occult, satanic and demon worship that's been on the Earth since the beginning. It's shiny new packaging to fool the masses. Not only in the world, but in the Church.

What used to be obvious as the occult and the association of demons has become widely accepted as the "enlightened" understanding of the spiritual realm.

WOO SPIRITUALITY

Woo spirituality refers to beliefs, practices, and systems that masquerade as profound spiritual truth while lacking a genuine divine foundation, biblical grounding, or even logical rationality. The term "Woo" (sometimes "Woo-woo") describes feel-good, mystical-sounding concepts that promise enlightenment, healing, or spiritual advancement through methods that bypass a genuine relationship with the One and Only, True God, personal responsibility, and biblical truth.

SPIRITUAL JUNK FOOD

Woo is spiritual junk food. It looks appealing, tastes sweet, gives you a quick high, and leaves you spiritually malnourished and crashing harder than before.

In the rebranding and repackaging of ancient occult, satanic, and demon worship, what used to be obviously evil has been given all these shiny new packages to fool the masses.

And guess who's buying it by the truckload? Christians. Because apparently, regular old prayer and Bible reading just isn't exciting enough anymore.

Why settle for a boring old relationship with the Creator of the universe when you can have crystal healing and angel encounters?

Woo is essentially *spiritual cotton candy*—colorful, sweet, instantly gratifying—but ultimately without substance. It attracts seekers with promises of secret knowledge, personal divinity, and consequence-free spirituality while leading them away from the narrow path as Jesus described.

THE SPIRITUAL SUGAR CRASH

You know what happens when you eat a bunch of sugar on an empty stomach first thing in the morning? First, you get what's called a "sugar high". You feel energized, awakened, empowered, ready to conquer the world.

Then comes the crash.

It's called the "mid-morning crash" when the sugar high and the false burst of energy wear off. Your blood sugar plummets. You get dizzy, headachy, exhausted. Your emotions go haywire. You hate everything and everyone around you. You're worse off than before you started.

Ever been there?

I have. A bunch of times.

Usually involving bad decisions that donuts are the breakfast of champions.

That's exactly how Woo works spiritually.

Woo is the "Sugar High"

At first, you feel amazing. Enlightened. Connected to spiritual realms that "regular" ol' people just don't understand. You feel more powerful, more awakened, more spiritually advanced than all those "dumb" Christians stuck in their religious boxes.

Yeah, those poor, unenlightened souls actually reading their Bibles and praying to the God who created the universe. How primitive.

But what happens when the "sugar high" wears off? When you crash down to reality? When you plummet to the bottom of the bottom? When you're worse off than you were before and you wake up wondering how the hell you got here?

This is what Woo will do to you.

Every. Single. Time.

STILL NOT CONVINCED? MEET YOUR SPIRITUAL DRUG DEALER

Still think Satan and his demons are your friendly neighborhood spirit guides? Still believe they're here to enlighten and empower you because you're so special?

Let me introduce you to your actual spiritual drug dealer. Spoiler alert: He's not as nice as your "ascended master" told you he was.

"You belong to your father, the devil, and you want to carry out your father's desires. **He was a murderer from the beginning**, not holding to the truth, for **there is NO truth in him**. When he lies, he speaks his native language, for he is a liar and the father of lies." (John 8:44)

"**The thief comes ONLY to steal** and **kill** and **destroy**; I have come that they may have life, and have it abundantly." (John 10:10)

So, he's a **MURDERER**. A **LIAR**. A **THIEF**. But hey, I'm sure he makes an exception for you because you found him through a really spiritual-sounding workshop.

He doesn't care about your enlightenment. He cares about your destruction.

He doesn't want to empower you. He wants to enslave you.

He doesn't want to heal you. He wants to kill you.

Are you still 100% certain the devil and his cohorts are here to give you protection and enlightenment?

I HOPE NOT

He's NEVER had your best interests at heart and NEVER will. And Woo is just his latest distribution method for spiritual poison.

THE VOCABULARY OF SPIRITUAL DECEPTION

The Anatomy of Woo: Recognizing the Counterfeit and the Language of Deception

This vocabulary gives the illusion and appearance of depth but disregards accountability for truth or morals.

Woo spirituality speaks its own special dialect. It's designed to sound really, really profound while saying absolutely nothing concrete. It's like spiritual word salad with extra mystical dressing.

Listen to the greatest hits and latest buzzwords: "Vibrations." "Energy." "Consciousness." "Manifestation." "Alignment." "The Universe." "Higher Self." "Divine Feminine." "Sacred Masculine." "Light Codes." "Frequency."

Notice what's mysteriously absent from this spiritual vocabulary? God. Jesus. Sin. Repentance. Salvation. Prayer. Obedience. Holiness. Truth.

Instead of sin, Woo practitioners talk about "shadow work" and "integration." Instead of repentance, they offer "healing." Instead of salvation through Jesus, they promote "ascension," "enlightenment," and "awakening."

How convenient. This linguistic sleight of hand allows people to feel spiritual without confronting their need for a Savior or dealing with that pesky accountability thing.

The Appeal to Ego

At its core, Woo spirituality appeals to humanity's oldest temptation—the desire, as the serpent promised Eve, "you will be like God." Modern Woo tells us we are divine beings who have forgotten our true nature. Teaching that we create our own reality. The universe exists to serve our desires. And we need no mediator between ourselves and the divine. Because we ARE divine.

This message proves irresistible to those who want spirituality without submission to God. Power without purity. Blessing without obedience. Woo promises you can have your spiritual cake and eat it too. No cross to bear. No flesh to crucify. No narrow gate to enter.

The only problem is that it's the same lie and the same deceiver. Just better marketing.

THE BILLION-DOLLAR SPIRITUAL CON GAME

Want to know how to spot a spiritual scam?

Easy.

Check the price tag.

Biblical spirituality — prayer, worship, Scripture reading, fellowship — costs absolutely nothing. But somehow, enlightenment always seems to require a credit card.

"Certified crystal healer" in a weekend—$500.

"Reiki Master" designation through an online course—$800.

"Spiritual life coach" certification—$2,000.

"Sacred activation" workshop—$1,500.

Nothing says "ancient wisdom" like a PayPal transaction and a laminated certificate.

They've turned spiritual exploitation into a multi-billion-dollar industry. They steal sacred ceremonies from other cultures, strip them of their original meaning, and then repackage and sell them to desperate Westerners looking for meaning in all the wrong places.

It's spiritual prostitution. And churches are becoming their biggest customers.

THE POISONOUS DOCTRINES OF WOO

The Law of Attraction Lie

Perhaps no Woo concept has infiltrated mainstream thinking more than the "Law of Attraction". Which promotes the idea that our thoughts create our reality and we can manifest whatever we desire through positive thinking and visualization.

"Think positive thoughts and manifest your reality."

"You create your own experience."

"The universe responds to your vibration."

Congratulations! You're now the god of your own little universe. How's that working out for you?

According to this brilliant doctrine, if you're poor, sick, or suffering, it's because you're thinking wrong, vibrating wrong, or manifesting wrong. It's all your fault. Negating that poverty, illness, and suffering result from living in a fallen world.

The Law of Attraction directly contradicts biblical teaching about suffering, perseverance, and God's sovereignty. It cannot explain why faithful believers suffer while the wicked prosper. It offers no comfort to the martyr. No hope for the persecuted. No meaning to trials that produce perseverance and character.

So go ahead and tell that to Job. Tell that to Paul in prison. Tell that to Jesus on the cross. Tell that to all the martyrs who gave their lives. I guess they just weren't thinking positively enough while being tortured for their faith.

(Impersonal) Universal Energy versus a Personal God

Woo spirituality is obsessed with "energy." Healing energy, negative energy, chakra energy, cosmic energy. Teaching this impersonal force flows through everything. You can manipulate it with crystals, cleanse it with sage, channel it through meditation, and proper alignment attracts it.

This energy concept replaces the personal God of Scripture with an impersonal force reminiscent of "Star Wars" spirituality—"May the Force be with you." You cannot have a relationship with energy. Energy doesn't love you. Energy didn't die for you. Energy offers no salvation. Energy is just a detached force that doesn't give a damn about your soul.

In Woo, it's a cosmic vending machine—insert the right practices, receive the desired outcome. This false mechanical spirituality strips the divine of personality, will, and moral character.

Turns out Yoda makes a terrible theologian.

Relativism ~ The "All Paths Lead to God" Lie

"Your truth" and "my truth" have replaced THE TRUTH in Woo

spirituality. "All beliefs are equally valid." "Every path leads to the same destination." And judgment becomes the only real sin people do.

This relativism sounds so tolerant and inclusive, doesn't it?

Yet, it shows its true colors in its intolerance, exclusion, and vehement denial of the possibility of a genuine singular Truth, when Jesus said, "I am THE Way, THE Truth, and THE Life. No one comes to the Father except through Me." (John 14:6)

Either Jesus was telling the truth, making Woo spirituality a deadly deception, or He was lying, making Christianity false.

Pick one.

There's no comfortable middle ground where everyone gets a participation trophy.

WOO WEARING A CHURCH MASK

The Infiltration of the Church: Woo in Sheep's Clothing

Here's where it gets really fun. The most dangerous Woo doesn't come from some crystal shop down the street. It comes from your own church, delivered by your own pastor / leader / minister / priest / bishop, wrapped in your own familiar Christian language.

"Christian" yoga. Contemplative prayer that empties your mind instead of filling it with Scripture. "Prophetic" painting channeled from "the Holy

Spirit." Crystal healing justified with references to temple stones. Destiny cards baptized as "prophecy cards."

Churches are hosting "manifestation" seminars, Enneagram workshops, and angel encounter sessions. Prosperity preachers have wholesale adopted the Law of Attraction—they just swapped "positive thinking" for "faith" and threw in some Bible verses for legitimacy.

Because apparently the gospel needed some improvements from the New Age movement.

When Movements Emphasize Experience Over Scripture

Some church movements have become breeding grounds for Christianized Woo. When you over-emphasize experience over Scripture, feelings over faith, and signs over substance, you create "spiritual junkies." Who are always seeking the next high, the next encounter, and the next manifestation. Instead of developing deep roots with God, His Word, His character, and learning how to walk with Him daily in His PEACE.

Where "Encounters," "Spiritual Portals and Atmospheres," "Grave Soaking," "Destiny Readings," "Angel orbs," and "Glory clouds" take precedence over sound doctrine. These are Woo practices that have somehow found acceptance in churches that claim to follow Jesus Christ and God the Father.

Which occurs when people yearn for spiritual connections, yet lack a strong biblical foundation. Which is vital to learn how to correctly "hear from God"—to distinguish His voice from all the others—as taught in *SET THE CAPTIVES FREE*.

This isn't Christianity.

This is witchcraft in a church building with better music and coffee.

WHAT WOO REALLY DOES TO YOUR SOUL

The Spiritual Consequences: You Opened Demonic Doors

Woo practices are like gateway drugs to the occult. What starts as "harmless" meditation or energy healing eventually progresses to channeling spirits, divination, and straight-up witchcraft.

Every former New Ager will tell you the same story: "It started so innocently..."

When you engage in practices that originate in pagan spirituality, you open doors God specifically commanded you to keep closed. The spiritual realm is real, and not all spirits come bearing gifts.

Actually, NONE of the fallen angels are friendly. ZERO. NADA. No matter what your "spirit guide" told you about himself.

Creates Spiritual Deception and Blindness

Engagement with Woo spirituality creates a special kind of spiritual blindness that makes recognizing the Truth increasingly difficult. When people have accepted darkness as light for long enough, real light starts looking like darkness to them. As a result, when they accept one deception, they become vulnerable to the next and the next. Ultimately, the discernment muscle atrophies through neglect—replaced by feelings and experiences as the arbiters of truth.

And here's the beautiful irony: This deception often comes with a false sense of enlightenment. People believe they've discovered "hidden truths," "secret knowledge," and "deeper spirituality" that makes them more spiritually advanced than those "primitive" Bible-believing Christians.

This pride becomes the perfect barrier to receiving genuine Truth. Why would you listen to simple gospel when you've got access to "cosmic consciousness"?

Produces No Real Transformation

Woo may generate temporary emotional highs, psychological comfort, or placebo effects. But it cannot address the fundamental human problem—our separation from God through sin. It can never provide a connection to the One and Only, True and Living God who created all.

Despite all its promises of personal growth, healing, and enlightenment, Woo spirituality produces ZERO lasting transformation. Want proof? Look at long-term practitioners.

Watch long-term practitioners of Woo spirituality, and you'll find people still struggling with the same issues, same sins, same brokenness—just with a spiritual vocabulary to mask it all.

Instead of transformation, they've learned to "accept themselves." Instead of crucifying their flesh, they've learned to "integrate their shadow." Instead of seeking God's Kingdom, they've learned to "manifest abundance." Sadly, these long-term practitioners are actually worse off than when they started. But their spiritual blindness keeps them convinced they're enlightened.

It's tragic.

TESTING THE SPIRITS:

THE FIVE-QUESTION WOO DETECTOR

All practices, teachings, and spiritual experiences must be measured by Scripture. And the scripture commands us to "Test the spirits to see whether they are from God." (1 John 4:1)

Good news: You don't need a theology degree to spot spiritual deception.

You just need five simple questions and a willingness to reject what fails the test—no matter how appealing it might seem:

1. **Does it acknowledge Jesus Christ alone as Lord?**

2. **Does it align with God's Word and biblical Truth?**

3. **Does it produce the fruit of the Spirit?**

4. **Does it draw people closer to God, the Father; or to themselves and other gods?**

5. **Does it produce God's PEACE that passes understanding (Philippians 4:7)?**

These questions can quickly expose Woo spirituality for what it is—a counterfeit that cannot withstand biblical scrutiny. If it fails any of these tests, reject it immediately.

Don't try to "redeem" it. Don't look for the good parts. Don't make excuses. Reject it completely and run.

Run. Fast.

Learn more about this subject in *SET THE CAPTIVES FREE*.

WHY SMART PEOPLE FALL FOR SPIRITUAL JUNK FOOD

Simple answer: People are desperately waiting for "feelings." Good feelings.

Why?

Due to their inner struggles, they don't feel good about themselves. No peace. No joy. No real love. They feel lifeless, empty, disconnected. So, they're constantly looking for something—anything—to fill the void.

The false spiritual world promises to fill them with good feelings. It tries to convince them they'll find answers through Woo. It's all about fixing you from the outside in.

But God's way is completely different—and a lot less immediately gratifying.

God fixes you from the inside first. That's where you find True Peace, True Joy, True Love, True Life—all coming from the inside out. And it's only possible through Jesus, the ONLY Door.

God doesn't play the Woo "feelings" games. He never will. He refuses to put on "a dog and pony show" to get your attention.

He's only interested in revealing Himself to people who become desperate enough to find Real Truth and are willing to abandon everything else to get it.

Even so, He's patient.

He's always there waiting for you when you're ready.

He's in no rush.

He has all eternity. But do you?

THE CHOICE: WOO OR TRUTH

The explosion of Woo spirituality in our culture reveals both massive danger and incredible opportunity. The danger is obvious: millions of people are being led straight to hell by beautiful, spiritual-sounding lies.

But the opportunity? The popularity of Woo proves people are spiritually hungry. They're looking for something real, something transcendent, something that connects them to the divine.

The choice between Woo and Truth is ultimately a choice between human wisdom and divine revelation. Between self-salvation and salvation through Christ. Between feeling good temporarily and being changed permanently.

We don't need crystals when we have Christ in us, the hope of glory. We don't need to manifest when we can pray. We don't need "the universe" when we have the Creator of the universe living in us.

Prayer, Scripture, fellowship, communion, worship—these might seem ordinary compared to Woo's exotic offerings. But they connect us to the genuine, all-powerful God who created everything and holds it all together by the word of His mouth.

In an age saturated with spiritual deception, we must have the courage to expose Woo for what it really is:

Evil's Great Masquerade

And then point seekers to the true Light that exists only in Jesus Christ.

CHAPTER SIX

SPIRITUAL DECEPTION DICTIONARY

BUZZWORDS AND BELIEFS THAT HAVE INFILTRATED AS ANGELS OF LIGHT

"I AM AFRAID THAT as the serpent deceived Eve by his cunning and craftiness, your thoughts and minds may be seduced, corrupted, and led astray from a wholehearted, sincere and pure devotion to Christ." (2 Corinthians 11:3)

A COMPREHENSIVE CATALOG OF MODERN FALSE SPIRITUAL PRACTICES

This is not intended to be an exhaustive catalog, as there are too many to fit into this book, and new names and definitions appear to grow by the day.

This is your field manual for identifying spiritual deception. Every term listed here represents a demonic counterfeit designed to seduce Christians away from biblical truth.

These aren't innocent spiritual practices. They're doorways to demonic influence. Each one leads people away from the True God and into the arms of lying spirits.

Use this as a reference manual. When you hear these terms in your church, your community, or from spiritual influencers or teachers, you'll know exactly what you're dealing with.

SPIRITUALITY REDEFINED

"Spirituality"—A deliberately vague term used to avoid accountability to any specific biblical doctrine. It creates the illusion of having a divine connection while rejecting biblical authority.

Translation: "I create my own god and live by my own rules."

"Spiritual but not religious"—Is the rejection of a biblical walk with the One and Only, True and Living God, while maintaining a belief in supernatural forces. It allows cherry-picking of appealing spiritual concepts without submission to divine authority or moral accountability.

Translation: "I don't need your God to find the true spiritual."

MANIFESTING DECEPTIONS

"Manifesting"—A belief that thoughts and intentions can directly alter physical reality. This attempts to use spiritual forces to serve personal desires rather than submitting to God's will. It's modern witchcraft disguised as positive thinking.

Translation: "You can create your own reality."

HEALING AND WELLNESS DECEPTIONS

"Healers" and "Light Workers"

What do "holistic health" and "holistic healer" mean in spiritual deception?

These practitioners claim to treat the whole person—body, mind, spirit, and emotions—rather than just physical symptoms. It considers lifestyle, nutrition, stress, relationships, and spiritual well-being as all being interconnected factors in health.

This intent seems to come from a good place.

But the practitioners within spiritual deception come from a dangerous place. The concern is in mixing the medical that cares about spiritual health as part of the whole person with obtaining spiritual help from the wrong spirits. It blurs the line between legitimate healthcare and wrong spiritual practices.

Here, those practitioners incorporate New Age, Eastern mysticism, and occult elements. They promote energy healing, chakras, crystals, and reiki while attributing healing to "universal energy" or "inner divinity" rather than God.

Creating source confusion—attributing healing to these outside forces—rather than on the One and Only, True God. Mixing Christianity with incompatible spiritual beliefs. Practitioners may claim spiritual powers or divine revelation outside of the Spirit of God or, worse, claim "their mixture" is from the Spirt of God Himself.

Note: God does not honor unholy mixtures. These practices open doors to demonic influence.

Some of the Red Flags to watch out for in Holistic Practice: Emphasis on "channeling energy"; references to spirit guides or ascended masters; claims about manipulating spiritual forces; and promoting the idea that humans are divine or can become god-like.

"Sound Healing" and Frequency Therapy

Claims frequencies, tones, and vibrations heal physical and emotional ailments by aligning "energy fields." Using sound baths with crystal bowls, gongs, and chimes. Using binaural beats and frequency therapy. Using solfeggio frequencies (claimed to be "sacred" healing tones). Vocal toning and humming for chakra alignment. And music therapy with "healing frequencies." These are based on occult beliefs about vibrational energy.

Which create altered states of consciousness that open practitioners to demonic influence—invoking spiritual entities through sound.

"Aromatherapy" with Spiritual

Components

Claims essential oils contain "spiritual properties" that can affect mood, consciousness, and spiritual well-being—going beyond their physical properties. Utilizing oils blessed by spiritual practitioners, or oils charged with "intentions." Promoting these oils "cleanse" spaces of negative energy.

"Grounding" and Earthing Practices

Claims direct physical contact with the Earth transfers beneficial energy and promotes spiritual connection with nature. Like: walking barefoot to connect with "Earth energy"; meditation while touching the ground; belief in receiving healing energy from the Earth; viewing the Earth as a conscious, spiritual entity. All combined with nature worship and paganism.

Often connected to New Age Earth worship and pantheistic beliefs that attribute consciousness and spiritual power to the creation—rather than honoring the Creator.

Body-Based Spiritual Practices

"Breathwork" and Conscious Breathing

Claims breathing techniques can induce spiritual experiences, emotional healing, and altered states of consciousness. Including: holotropic breathwork (developed by LSD researchers); rebirthing breathwork—claiming to heal birth trauma; the Wim Hof method (when used for spiritual purposes); pranayama and yogic breathing techniques; and breathwork combined with psychedelic experiences.

The Danger is in hyperventilation and breath manipulation—creating altered states.

"Somatic Therapy" with Spiritual Elements

Claims the body holds spiritual and emotional trauma, which is released through specific physical techniques and energy work. Promotes energy release through body manipulation. Accessing "cellular memory" and past-life trauma. Combining massage with energy healing. Using touch to manipulate spiritual energies. Based on the belief that emotions are stored in specific body parts.

Emotional healing comes through learning God's Word, forgiveness, and the Holy Spirit's work.

Not through manipulating supposed energy fields.

DIVINATION AND FORTUNE-TELLING

Modern Divination Practices

"Oracle Cards" and Angel Cards

Card decks claiming to provide spiritual guidance from angels, ascended masters, or "universal intelligence."

Popular variations include "angel oracle cards" claiming messages from angels. "Goddess cards" connecting with "feminine divine energy." "Animal spirit cards" for shamanic guidance. "Affirmation cards" with metaphysical concepts. And "archetype cards" based on Jungian psychology mixed with occultism.

ALL are forms of divination seeking supernatural connections and knowledge through familiar spirits posing as angels or guides.

God has forbidden ALL divination, regardless of (re) packaging.

"Pendulum Dowsing" and Muscle Testing

Using pendulums or applied kinesiology (muscle testing) to reveal hidden knowledge, detect energy imbalances, or to make decisions. Advocating pendulums or muscle weakness / responses are able to answer Yes / No questions. Utilizes dowsing for water, lost objects, or spiritual information. Muscle testing for food sensitivities with spiritual interpretation. Muscle testing / weakness / responses / reactions back promoted metaphysical beliefs—promoting spiritual truth is learned through physical responses.

"And when the people [instead of putting their trust in God] shall say to you, consult for direction mediums and wizards [who chirp and mutter], should not a people seek and consult their God? Should they consult the dead on behalf of the living?" (Isaiah 8:19)

"Numerology" and Sacred Geometry

Claims numbers and geometric patterns contain mystical significance and reveal spiritual truths about personality, destiny, and reality. Believing life path numbers determine personality and destiny. Angel numbers provide spiritual messages. Sacred geometry as divine communication. Applying gematria and biblical numerology to find hidden meanings. Creating architectural designs based on spiritual geometry.

God does use numbers as symbols and types in Scripture.

Numerology attempts to gain some kind of additional supernatural knowledge through mathematical formulas—rather than divine revelation.

Technology-Enhanced Divination such as "Spiritual Apps" and Digital Guidance

Claims Smartphone Apps can provide spiritual guidance, energy readings, and metaphysical insights. Daily card pulls from oracle or other spiritual card decks. Astrology Apps for daily readings. Meditation Apps with Eastern mysticism. Chakra balancing and energy reading Apps. Crystal identification and healing Apps. With more Apps being added by the day.

Technology CANNOT provide spiritual guidance.

These Apps either generate random responses or connect users to spiritual deceptions, and worse, actual spirits through digital means.

"Biofeedback" with Spiritual Interpretation

Claims electronic devices measure spiritual energy, auras, and metaphysical health conditions. Aura photography shows spiritual energy. Utilizes biofeedback machines to measure "spiritual frequencies." Radionics devices for distant healing. Claims of diagnosing and treat health conditions by detecting and manipulating electromagnetic frequencies or "subtle energies" in the body. Using Kirlian photography for energy field detection. And computer programs used to analyze spiritual compatibility.

CONSCIOUSNESS AND

REALITY MANIPULATION

Advanced Manifestation Techniques like "Timeline Jumping" and Parallel Reality Access

Claims consciousness access and shifts between alternate timelines and parallel versions of reality. Utilizes visualization techniques for timeline shifting. Access to "higher dimensional" versions of yourself. Quantum jumping between probable realities. Retroactive manifestation to change past events. Accessing dimensional portals and reality gates.

This represents the ultimate in reality dissociation and can lead to severe mental instability, psychotic episodes, and, opens the participants to demonic influence.

"Akashic Records" Access

Claims a mystical library in the spiritual realm, which contains all knowledge of past, present, and future—only accessible through meditation and spiritual techniques. Reading past lives and soul contracts. Accessing information about future events. Receiving guidance from "record keepers." Learning soul purposes and spiritual missions. Stating you can clear karmic debt through record work.

This is divination and spirit contact disguised as spiritual research. Information received comes from familiar spirits, not cosmic libraries.

This is no different from accessing the same type of information from physics and mediums of the past.

"DNA Activation" and Genetic Upgrading

Claims humans can activate dormant spiritual DNA strands through energy work and consciousness techniques. Activation of 12-strand DNA for spiritual evolution. Backing the New Age belief that humans have 10 "dormant" or "etheric" DNA strands beyond the two physical ones. Upgrading genetic codes through energy healing. Removing genetic blocks to spiritual advancement. Installing new DNA templates from higher dimensions. Allowing us to become multidimensional through genetic activation.

Misusing genetic science to support New Age beliefs about human evolution and spiritual advancement.

Claiming participants will achieve a higher state of consciousness and psychic abilities; connections to higher dimensions; ascension and spiritual evolution; along with healing and longevity.

Collective Consciousness Practices

Such as "Global Consciousness" and Mass Meditation Events

Claims group meditation and consciousness work influence global events and raise planetary vibration. Global meditation for world peace—with mass consciousness experiments. Planetary gridwork and energy transmission. Collective intention for environmental healing. Synchronized meditation for spiritual awakening.

While prayer for the world is biblical, these practices often involve invoking spiritual entities and attempting to manipulate reality through group consciousness rather than submitting to God's sovereignty.

Unfortunately, these flawed efforts will only be answered by the wrong spiritual forces.

"Starseed" and Alien Spirituality

Claims some humans are actually spiritual beings from other planets or dimensions—who have been incarnated on Earth for spiritual missions. Self identifying as Pleiadian, Arcturian, or other "star races." Receiving messages from galactic councils to share with other mere humans. Preparing for ascension events and planet evacuation. DNA upgrades from extraterrestrial sources. They're here for mission work as "lightworkers" for planetary transformation.

This is an extreme form of dissociation from human identity and often

Involves contact with demonic entities posing as alien beings.

TRAUMA AND THERAPY DECEPTIONS

"Past Life Regression" Therapy

Claims current problems are healed by accessing and resolving issues from previous incarnations. Phobias and relationship patterns come from past-life trauma—healed through past-life trauma resolution. Relationship patterns can be understood through past-life connections. Releases karmic debt and soul contracts. Accessing talents and abilities from previous lives. Healing physical ailments with past-life origins.

It involves spirit contact and demonic deception about human identity and eternal destiny.

"Soul Retrieval" and Shamanic Healing

Claims traumas cause soul fragments to separate within you and must be retrieved through shamanic journey work. Uses drumming to induce altered states; spirit guide assistance in soul retrieval; power animal recovery for spiritual protection; extraction of spiritual intrusions and curses; and cord-cutting ceremonies for relationship healing.

It involves direct contact with familiar spirits and can create severe spiritual oppression.

Energy Psychology and Tapping Methods

Such as "EFT" (Emotional Freedom Technique) with Spiritual Elements

Claims tapping on meridian points while speaking affirmations clear emotional and spiritual blockages. Includes tapping while invoking spiritual guides or angels; clearing past life trauma through EFT; using EFT for chakra balancing and energy work; combining with manifestation and attraction techniques; and testing for spiritual blocks through muscle testing.

While some might believe basic EFT to have psychological benefits — spiritual applications involve energy manipulation and occult beliefs about meridian systems.

Tapping into the wrong spirits who will be glad to create

havoc in the participants.

"EMDR" [Eye Movement Desensitization and Reprocessing] with Metaphysical Additions

Claims eye movement therapy is enhanced with spiritual visualization and energy work for deeper healing. Encouraging visualization of spiritual guides during sessions. Accessing past lives through EMDR protocols. Being able to install positive spiritual experiences to replace the negative ones. Clearing generational curses through eye movements. Combining EMDR with energy healing and chakra work enhances the results.

Again, tapping into the wrong spirits who will gladly create chaos.

RELATIONSHIP AND SEXUALITY DECEPTIONS

"For this is the will of God, your sanctification; that is, that you abstain from sexual immorality." (1 Thessalonians 4:3-5)

"Sacred Sexuality" and Divine Union

Claims sexual practices are spiritual pathways to divine consciousness and energy exchange. Tantra as a spiritual practice for consciousness expansion. Sex magic and energy exchange between partners. Sacred prostitution and temple sexuality. Polyamory as spiritual evolution. Sexual chakra work and kundalini activation. Believing they create profound spiritual experiences and transformations—including increased awareness and emotional healing.

"Twin Flame" and Soul Mate Mythology

Claims each person has a perfect spiritual counterpart, and finding this person is essential for spiritual completion. Promotes leaving marriages to find "true" twin flames. Believes ALL current relationships are spiritually inferior until you find the ONE. Waiting on cosmic timing to unite with soul-mates. Utilizes past-life connections to determine current relationships. Promoting sexual relationships as spiritual advancement.

Destroys biblical marriage and creates unrealistic expectations that prevent genuine relationship satisfaction.

"Divine Feminine" / "Divine Masculine" Energy Work

Claims all beings contain both feminine and masculine divine energies—requiring balance for spiritual wholeness. Includes goddess worship and divine feminine rituals. Sacred masculine energy work and men's circles. Gender fluidity as spiritual evolution. Balancing the inner feminine and masculine through meditation. Applying moon cycles and goddess energy connections.

While God did create male and female,

Attributing divine characteristics to gender energies leads to confusion about biblical sexuality and opens doors to occult practices.

DEATH AND AFTERLIFE DECEPTIONS

"Mediumship" and Channeling the Dead

Claims gifted individuals can communicate with spirits of the deceased for comfort and guidance. Such as psychic mediums to contact deceased relatives. Channeling ascended masters, spiritual teachers, and automatic writing from spirit guides. Using electronic voice phenomena (EVP) for spirit communication. With séances and spirit circles for group communication.

This is nothing more than a repackaging of the old.

Physics, mediums, séances, and spiritualism from the past to access false spirits who will ALWAYS answer the deception.

"Near-Death Experience" Theology

Claims near-death experiences provide authoritative information about the afterlife that supersedes biblical teaching. Advocating universal salvation is the actual truth based on NDE reports. And there are "multiple paths to heaven" confirmed by such experiences. Championing reincarnation is validated through life reviews. Recommending New Age afterlife descriptions replace biblical truth.

NDE experiences are considered a higher revelation than Scripture.

While NDEs may be real experiences, they must be interpreted through Scripture rather than used to reinterpret biblical truth about eternity.

"Ancestral Healing" and Generational Work

Claims ancestors can be contacted for healing and guidance to influence living descendants. Advocating altar creation for deceased family members—offering food and gifts to ancestral spirits—looking for their advice. Expecting healing of generational trauma through ancestor communication. Honoring ancestors through ritual and ceremony.

This is necromancy and involves familiar spirits posing as deceased relatives.

PLANT MEDICINE AND PSYCHEDELIC SPIRITUALITY

"Ayahuasca" and Plant Spirit Medicine

Claims psychedelic plants contain spiritual intelligence and can provide healing, guidance, and spiritual awakening. Promoting ayahuasca ceremonies with shamanic guidance. Using psilocybin mushrooms for spiritual breakthrough and psychedelic DMT (dimethyltryptamine) experiences as spiritual travel. Advocating peyote and mescaline for vision quests. And cannabis for spiritual sacrament and consciousness expansion.

Psychedelic experiences involve direct contact with demonic entities presenting themselves as plant spirits, guides, or divine beings.

Partaking in these experiences creates lasting spiritual

bondage and mental instability.

"Microdosing" for Spiritual Enhancement

Claiming it's completely safe to consume small doses of psychedelic substances to enhance creativity, spirituality, and consciousness with no need to experience full hallucinogenic effects.

Yet again, it needs to be understood that even small amounts of psychedelic substances open the wrong spiritual doors, as well as create a dependency on chemical means for spiritual experience,

Rather than finding a personal relationship with God.

Sacred Plant Traditions: "Cannabis Spirituality" and Marijuana Ministry

Claims cannabis is a sacred plant that can enhance spiritual experiences, meditation, and connection with the divine. Creating cannabis churches and marijuana ministries. Utilizes marijuana for enhanced prayer and worship. Cannabis as a biblical herb for spiritual use. Advocating THC and CBD for spiritual healing and consciousness.

Combining marijuana with Christian meditation as a way to reach God.

While marijuana may have some valid medical applications, using mind-altering substances for spiritual purposes represents seeking spiritual experience through chemical means rather than the Holy Spirit.

When done, it opens the users to the wrong spirits—not to God.

BUSINESS AND PROSPERITY DECEPTIONS

Spiritual Business and Manifestation: "Spiritual Entrepreneurship" and Conscious Business

Claims business is a perfect place to practice "spiritual manifestation" — using manifestation techniques to attract success. Incorporating chakra work and energy healing into business plans. Using moon phases and astrology for business timing. Applying crystal grids and Feng Shui for business prosperity. Instructing spiritual coaching for "soul-aligned" business success.

Mixes legitimate business principles with occult practices, creating dependency on spiritual manipulation rather than wise business practices and God's blessing.

"Network Marketing" with Spiritual Elements

Teaches MLM businesses how to sell spiritual products or services as vehicles for both financial and spiritual advancement. Advocating essential oil companies making spiritual claims; crystal and gemstone MLMs; energy healing certification programs; spiritual coaching and life coaching MLMs; and wellness products with metaphysical marketing.

These businesses create financial exploitation while spreading spiritual deception through their products and training.

CHILDREN AND FAMILY DECEPTIONS

Spiritual Parenting and Child Development: "Indigo/Crystal/Rainbow Children"

Claims some children are spiritually advanced beings with special psychic abilities and spiritual missions. Advocating children with ADHD or autism are actually spiritually gifted. Being able to see auras, spirits, and energy fields. Discourages discipline and traditional education as spiritually suppressive—damaging their gifts and spiritual abilities. Recommends parents encourage children's psychic experiences.

Prevents proper diagnosis and treatment while opening children to spiritual deception and demonic influence.

"Conscious Parenting" with New Age Elements

Promotes parents guide their children's spiritual development through metaphysical practices—while avoiding traditional biblical restrictions. Advocating children's meditation and visualization techniques. Encouraging children to seek "their spirit guides" and "angels." Using crystals and energy work. Avoiding biblical concepts of sin and salvation—claiming that will limit their connection into the expanded spiritual realm available to them. Encouraging spiritual experimentation without biblical boundaries.

This opens children to spiritual deception and demonic influence from a young age.

Educational Deceptions: "Waldorf/Steiner Education" with Anthroposophical Roots

Claims education should develop children's spiritual nature through anthroposophical principles, including reincarnation and spiritual evolution. Promoting "seven-year developmental cycles" based on their spiritual evolution. Advocating the eurythmy movement as spiritual development. Delaying academic learning based on the child's spiritual readiness. Attending seasonal festivals with mixed pagan and Christian traditions. Finding teachers for your children trained in anthroposophical spiritual development.

The underlying spiritual philosophy contradicts biblical truth about human nature and spiritual development.

Again, opening children to spiritual deception and demonic influence.

COMMUNITY AND SOCIAL DECEPTIONS

Spiritual Communities: "Ecovillages" and Sustainable Spirituality

Claims environmental sustainability requires spiritual practices honoring

Earth as a conscious divine entity. Promotes Earth worship, Gaia consciousness, Earth-based spirituality, and "high vibration" (energetically charged) food. Living in harmony with "universal energy flows" and "Healing the Earth." Communal living based on spiritual principles. Consensus decision-making through spiritual guidance. With integration of other spiritual traditions and practices.

While environmental stewardship is biblical, these communities promote Earth worship, contradicting Scripture.

"Rainbow Gatherings" and Spiritual Festivals

Claim large gatherings of spiritually minded people create collective consciousness, promoting peace and love. Recommends group meditation and consciousness raising. Sharing spiritual practices and teachings. Encourages creation of spiritual communities. Champions environmental activism with spiritual motivations.

These gatherings promote spiritual syncretism; often involve drug use and occult practices for spiritual experiences and consciousness expansion.

Creates spiritual dangers through these practices.

THE EXPANDING NATURE OF SPIRITUAL DECEPTION

Why This List Continues to Grow

The catalog of spiritual deceptions continues to expand for many reasons:

First: Cultural acceptance. Society increasingly normalizes these occult, spiritual, and Woo practices as wellness and self-improvement.

Second: Technological integration. New technologies continue to create new platforms for spreading spiritual deception.

Third: Generational shifts. Each generation continues to repackage ancient deceptions in new contemporary forms.

Fourth: Market demands. Spiritual seeking creates profitable markets for deceptive products and services.

And Fifth: Educational infiltration. Schools and universities promote Eastern mysticism, New Age concepts, and other spiritual Woo as normal.

STAYING ALERT

Staying Current with Emerging Deceptions and Ongoing Discernment

Study: Contemporary spiritual trends through a biblical lens.

Monitor: Popular wellness and self-help movements for spiritual elements.

Research: New therapeutic modalities for metaphysical components.

Evaluate: Children's entertainment and education for spiritual content.

Stay Informed: About technological applications with spiritual claims.

THE PATTERN

Did you notice a pattern yet?

Every single one of these promises knowledge, power, or insight from somewhere other than God.

[Who knew?] Almost like there's an agenda or something.

Creating altered states, opening practitioners to spiritual deception.

We need to recognize that true knowledge and healing come through learning God's Word, forgiveness, and the Holy Spirit's work in us. Not through manipulating supposed energy fields or getting revelation from "spirits," their representatives, space, the heavens or the Earth.

FINAL WARNING

EVERY Practice Listed Opens a Doorway to Demonic Influence.

NONE ARE HARMLESS.

ALL Lead Away from the One True God.

CHAPTER SEVEN

UNDERSTANDING THE SPIRITUAL BATTLEFIELD

THE FOUR COMPETING VOICES

"The Largest Area of Captivity is Between the Ears"

The Mind is the Battlefield

Y OUR MIND IS NOT neutral territory. Every moment of every day, four distinct voices compete for control of your thoughts, decisions, and ultimately, your destiny. Most Christians have never received proper training to distinguish between these voices. They're sitting ducks for spiritual deception and manipulation.

The enemy doesn't need to possess you when he's already programmed you to run his maze like a trained mouse. Why bother with dramatic possession when subtle programming works so much better?

As the god of this world, Satan and his minions have overseen us from the time we were born. We grew up under his tutelage. We knew no other way. We had no other option. He trained us perfectly to do all he wanted. He instilled in us from the beginning our old nature, the old man, the flesh, and trained us to listen and respond to him.

Therefore, understanding these four voices is the foundation of all spiritual discernment and the first step toward authentic freedom. I explain these things in great detail in **SET THE CAPTIVES FREE**, but will review them in part here.

Identifying the Four Competing Voices

Think of your mind as a radio picking up four different stations broadcasting simultaneously. Most people spend their entire lives never learning how to tune into the right frequency.

First: GOD'S Still Small Quiet Voice

We're told in the Word that we can all hear the still small voice of God from within. On the day of our salvation, we were SEALED with the promised Holy Spirit (the Anointing). (Ephesians 1:13; 2 Corinthians 1:21–22)

Therefore, for all believers, the Holy Spirit (the Anointing) resides in our spirit, and if we yield, He will flow through our soul, and if we yield more, through our body, and beyond. These are the rivers of living water that will come out of our innermost being when we yield and get out of the way. (John 7:38-39)

First Kings 19:11–12 tells us, "But the Lord was **NOT** in the wind; and after the wind, an earthquake, but the Lord was **NOT** in the earthquake; and after the earthquake, a fire, but the Lord was **NOT** in the fire; and after the fire [a sound of Gentle Stillness] **A STILL, SMALL VOICE.**" And in Psalm 46:10, we're told, "Be still, and know that I AM God."

God's voice is typically not audible. It's not dramatic. It doesn't compete for attention like a carnival barker. Which explains why most people miss it completely. We're too busy, too distracted, too addicted to noise and chaos to hear the gentle whisper of the Creator.

But we need to learn to be still.

Then, learn to listen. Carefully. Correctly.

What are the characteristics of His voice?

How do we learn to distinguish His voice from the others?

By His PEACE.

Not "a peace". Only **THE PEACE** that passes comprehension and understanding. That **PEACE** aligns perfectly with Scripture. It promotes His perfect love, joy, hope, and faith. It builds up rather than tears down. It leads to freedom and life. It often comes with gentle conviction, not condemnation.

"And **THE PEACE** of God, which surpasses all understanding [comprehension], will guard your hearts and your minds in Christ [the Anointing] Jesus." (Philippians 4:7)

This is the Only characteristic that can guide us. It's something that the enemy and his minions cannot reproduce. They can give "a peace"—but don't mistake "a peace" for "**THE PEACE.**" Learn more in *THE DAILY*

STAND.

How God Speaks

First: Through His written Word (Scripture). But as shown in *THE DAILY STAND*, Satan knows God's word better than we do, so that's not enough.

Second: Through the Holy Spirit's inner witness.

Third: Through His still small voice.

Fourth: (Sometimes) Through circumstances aligned with His will. As well as through mature believers speaking biblical truth. These things must be confirmed by the next and most important way.

Fifth: Through that DEEP, incomparable **PEACE** that ONLY He can give that CONFIRMS His guidance.

"My sheep hear my voice, and I know them, and they follow me." (John 10:27)

Second: Satan's Voice

What are the Characteristics of Satan or his minions' voices we hear?

First and foremost, it's always based on deception. Hiding under masks. Acting like it's helping—but deceiving you even more. Pretending it's bringing good, while **ALL** the time taking you deeper into more profound deceit. Eventually, it will show its true nature.

It brings fear, condemnation, and confusion.

It contradicts or twists Scripture.

It promotes pride, lust, greed, and hatred.

It tears down and destroys.

It leads to deeper deception.

It leads to bondage and death.

It often comes with accusations and hopelessness.

Always Remember:

Until we ask the Lord to come into our lives, this is the voice we were raised with. We knew nothing different—nothing better. Therefore, this is deeply ingrained in our psyche—and throughout our whole person.

Satan has been our primary spiritual mentor since birth. Kind of puts those "trust your heart" and "follow your instincts" philosophies in perspective, doesn't it?

How Satan Speaks

Through masks pretending to be "light"—which enables him and his cohorts to speak:

Through direct lies and deception.

Through twisting Scripture out of context.

Through cultural influences that oppose biblical truth.

Through demonic spirits, false angels, and false spiritual experiences.

Through that nagging voice of condemnation and fear.

"He was a **murderer from the beginning**, and does **NOT stand in the Truth**, because **there is NO Truth in him**. When he lies, he speaks out of his own character, for he is a liar and the father of lies." (John 8:44)

Third: Your Own Voice

What are its Characteristics?

It reflects your emotions, desires, and reasoning.

It can be influenced by past experiences and trauma.

It's often driven by self-interest and immediate gratification.

It may sound reasonable, but lacks spiritual wisdom.

It can be positive or negative, depending on your spiritual condition.

This is the voice that tells you the chocolate cake is a good idea at 12 midnight, that you deserve to buy things you can't afford, and that your ex was probably "the one."

Sources of Your Voice

Flesh and carnal nature.

Emotional responses to circumstances.

Past programming and experiences.

Human reasoning apart from God's wisdom.

Unhealed wounds and trauma responses.

Even though these things are ALL valid influences. We MUST understand, most importantly, that **ALL** of our training in this world came from the devil, the god of this world. As stated, he raised us from the very beginning, and we are merely mice that have learned to run his maze.

"The heart is deceitful above all things, and desperately sick; who can understand it?" (Jeremiah 17:9)

So you've got one blind person asking another blind person for directions, and they're both following a map drawn by someone who wants them to fall into a pit. How will that work out for them?

Fourth: Others' Voices

What are their Characteristics?

They can include family, friends, culture, and media influence.

It can be positive or negative depending on the source.

It often carries emotional weight due to relationships.

It may contradict your personal convictions.

It can create pressure to conform or rebel.

Sources of Others' Voices

Family expectations and traditions.

Peer pressure and social influence.

Cultural norms and media messages.

Religious leaders and spiritual authorities.

Professional and educational influences.

Yet again, and most importantly, we need to understand that **ALL** of their training came from the devil as the god of this world. He raised them from the very beginning, and they also, are merely mice that have learned to run his maze.

"Do not be conformed to this world, but be transformed by the renewal of your mind." (Romans 12:2)

WHAT WE SHOULD LEARN WHEN KEEPING ALL THESE SOURCES IN MIND

Three of the four voices we hear are wrong.

And those voices are the loudest—yelling in our ears, minds, and emotions—all day long. **ALL** coming from the same "well." Whether it's the devil and his minions speaking directly to us—or ourselves—or others influencing us; **ALL** trained by him.

The hardest to hear is from God Himself. Not that He's incapable of being the loudest in the room or drowning out the other three. But by design, He'll always be the quietest in the room. Only those who choose to seek Him above all else will find Him. Then,

"As the deer pants for streams of water, so my soul pants for you, my God." (Psalm 42:1)

"Those who seek me diligently will find me." (Proverbs 8:17)

"You will seek me and find me when you seek me with all your heart." (Jeremiah 29:13)

And, "Seek and you will find; knock and the door will be opened." (Matthew 7:7)

THE TRAINING MOST CHRISTIANS NEVER

RECEIVED

Why We're Vulnerable

First: We have a lack of proper teaching. Most churches don't train believers in spiritual discernment. It's like sending soldiers into battle without teaching them to distinguish between their own troops and enemy forces.

Second: There's the environment of cultural Christianity. We have surface-level faith without a deep biblical foundation and a deep personal relationship with the Father.

Third: We have emotional decision-making. We prioritize feelings over Scripture.

Fourth: Spiritual laziness. We want others to hear God for us. Whether it's pastors, leaders, ministers, priests, or even other believers. Just as Israel sent Moses up the mountain to hear God for them.

Fifth: Pride. We [mistakenly] believe we can easily distinguish God's voice without training.

The Default Pattern

When untrained in discernment, most believers default to: Following their emotions (their own voice). Accepting whatever sounds and feels good (often Satan's deception). Conforming to social pressure (others' voices). And missing God's gentle, still small voice altogether.

The last is the hardest to do. It takes a deep commitment to learn the Scriptures, learn THE PEACE of God, learn how to walk in the Spirit, and learn how to lean into the Father all the time. Prioritizing Him and His Word over everything else.

The "Trained Mice" Phenomenon

How the Enemy Programs Believers and Non-Believers Alike

First: Similar to laboratory mice running a maze for rewards, people can be programmed to follow predictable patterns.

Second: By creating false reward systems. Promising spiritual experiences, material blessings, and social acceptance for following certain paths.

Third: By establishing familiar patterns. Making deception feel comfortable and "normal."

Fourth: By providing counterfeit confirmations. Offering a false peace or temporary benefits to reinforce wrong choices.

Fifth: By punishing deviation. Creating fear, guilt, or social pressure when anyone questions the system.

Common Spiritual Mazes

First: The religious performance maze. Running endless activities to earn God's approval.

Second: The prosperity maze. Chasing material blessings as evidence of spiritual success.

Third: The experience maze. Seeking supernatural experiences as proof of God's presence.

Fourth: The knowledge maze. Accumulating information without transformation.

Fifth: The ministry maze. Finding identity in serving rather than being

God's child and walking daily, intimately with Him.

Christians run these religious mazes—always looking for the next spiritual cheese.

LEARNING TO DISTINGUISH THE VOICES

THE PEACE of God Test

The primary test for God's voice is "**THE PEACE** of God that passes understanding"—as we saw in Philippians 4:7. This isn't just any type of peace, but God's specific **PEACE** that:

Remains steady despite circumstances—even during the greatest storms of life.

Increases as you move toward God's will.

Brings clarity and confidence.

Always aligns with Biblical Truth.

And, Always produces lasting fruit.

The Scripture Test

God will speak nothing that contradicts His written

Word / Bible / Scripture.

Compare every spiritual impression with Scripture.

Study the context and original texts. Not just isolated verses. Not with a singular version that you were told was the ONLY correct one.

Seek understanding alongside other mature biblical believers.

Test all interpretations against the whole counsel of God—which is always the combination of His Word along with His PEACE.

The Fruit Test

"By their fruits you will know them." (Matthew 7:16)

God's voice produces:

Love, joy, peace, patience, kindness, goodness, faithfulness, gentleness, and self-control.

Satan's voice, both directly and through what has been imparted in us or others, produces:

Fear, anger, pride, lust, greed, hatred, division, confusion, and bondage.

The Humility Test

God's voice promotes humility and dependence on Him.

Acknowledges "we only see, hear, and know in part."

Says "I sense" or "I believe" rather than "Thus says the Lord."

Seeks confirmation through Scripture and mature counsel.

Remains open to correction and adjustment.

To learn more about this vitally important subject, read about this in ***SET THE CAPTIVES FREE***.

THE NATURE OF SPIRITUAL DECEPTION

"The Beautiful Side of Evil" — Understanding the Enemy's Strategy

Spiritual deception is never ugly, obvious, or repulsive—if it were, no one would fall for it. The most dangerous deceptions come packaged in beautiful, appealing, seemingly beneficial forms that meet real human needs while leading people away from God's Truth.

Satan's primary strategy has remained unchanged since the Garden of Eden. Presenting only enough truth—whatever is needed to convince the listener—then mix with his lies to take people off-course, away from God. Then present rebellion against God as beneficial, enlightening, and liberating.

Every spiritual deception contains enough truth to be believable and enough appeal to be desirable—while containing enough poison to be deadly.

New Age: "Is Jesus the only way?"

Liberal Theology: "If God is love, wouldn't He accept all expressions of love?"

Same serpent.

Same lie.

Different generation.

Same results.

The Original Genesis Deception (Genesis 3:1-6)

Every spiritual deception follows the pattern established in Eden.

First: Question God's Word: "Can it really be that God said...?"

Next: Deny God's Consequences: "You surely will not die!"

Third: Promise divine benefits: "God knows that in the day you eat from it your eyes will be opened, and you will be like God, knowing good and evil."

And Fourth: Appeal to human desires: "[It's] good for food and pleasing to the eye, and also desirable to make one wise."

MODERN APPLICATIONS OF THE GENESIS PATTERN

Let's look at "New Age" and other "Woo spirituality".

"Has God really said Jesus is the only way?"

"You can become divine through many spiritual practices."

"Why would God want you to limit finding out every way you could know Him in the spiritual realm?"

"You know the bible was written by men and we can't take it literally, so don't limit yourself like other dogmatic religious people do."

"Eventually, you'll be like God and can help others come to know Him better by all you've learned."

"You're not just doing this for yourself, you're doing this to help the ones you love and many others."

How about the "Prosperity Gospel?"

"Has God really said to be content?"

"You deserve abundant material blessings."

"Didn't Jesus instruct us to 'ask for anything in My name and My Father will do it for you?'"

"Didn't Jesus also instruct us to use OUR Faith and just Believe and ALL these things will be added to you?"

"Don't you think God wants the Very Best for His children?"

"Why should anyone believe those people who don't operate in Faith, like we do, and limit what we can achieve with God?"

"And besides, God said He's preparing a place for us where the streets are lined with gold!"

How about in "Liberal Theology?"

"Has God really said homosexuality is a sin?"

[Again, remembering] "The bible was written by men so we can't take it literally—don't limit yourself like other dogmatic religious people do."

"If God is Love, then wouldn't God's Love everyone, no matter what?"

"Wouldn't He be so glad people are promoting Love verses hate?"

"And openly accepts all expressions of sexuality?"

Then there's "Manifestation Teachings."

"Has God really said to submit to His will alone?"

"Do you think that God is limited by men and their teachings?"

"Didn't God say 'if you have Faith and Believe' that you can manifest anything, including telling a mountain to move itself into the sea?"

"He wants you to learn to Believe and make things become reality."

"He wants you to grow up and be like Him."

"Didn't He just visualize the world coming into being and then just manifested it in six days?"

"You're a child of God—you can create your own reality."

THE COMMON PILLARS OF SPIRITUAL DECEPTION

First is the Promise of Self-Deification

The Promise: "You can become like God."

The Appeal: Ultimate power and control over your circumstances.

The Reality: Is pride-based rebellion that separates you from the True God.

Because that worked out so well for Lucifer, right?

Modern Examples:

"You are a divine being having a human experience."

"You have unlimited creative power within you."

"Tap into your inner goddess/god."

"You create your own reality."

Biblical Response:

"Before me no god was formed, nor shall there be any after me." (Isaiah 43:10)

Second is the Rejection of Biblical Authority

The Promise: "You don't need external religious authority from God or men."

The Appeal: Is freedom from moral constraints and religious rules.

The Reality: Is creating personal spiritual systems that serve the flesh.

Modern Examples:

"I'm spiritual but not religious."

"All paths lead to God."

"Trust your inner wisdom and other ancient books more than just the Bible."

"Create your own truth."

Biblical Response:

"Sanctify them by the Truth; Your Word is Truth." (John 17:17)

And again, "Jesus said to him, I am the Way and the Truth and the Life; no one comes to the Father except by (through) Me." (John 14:6)

Third is Pride-Based Appeal

The Promise: "You can achieve spiritual superiority."

The Appeal: Is feeling special, enlightened, or more advanced than others.

The Reality: Is spiritual pride that opposes God's Grace.

Nothing feeds the ego like believing you're part of the spiritually elite while everyone else is stuck in "primitive" religious thinking.

Modern Examples:

"You're more spiritually evolved than traditional Christians."

"You have special gifts that others don't understand."

"You've awakened while others remain asleep."

"You're part of the chosen few who understand truth."

Biblical Response:

"God opposes the proud but gives grace to the humble." (James 4:6)

Fourth is Experience-Driven Validation

The Promise: "Spiritual experiences prove the truth you're on the right path."

The Appeal: Is supernatural encounters that feel powerful and real.

The Reality: Is demonic counterfeits can produce impressive experiences.

Modern Examples:

"I felt such a peace during crystal meditation."

"My chakras opened and I felt divine energy."

"I contacted my spirit guide who gave me wisdom."

"The universe confirmed my manifestation with signs."

Biblical Response:

"Beloved, do not believe every spirit, but test the spirits to see whether they are from God." (1 John 4:1)

Fifth is Syncretistic Mixtures

The Promise: "You can combine the best of all spiritual traditions."

The Appeal: Is cherry-picking appealing elements while avoiding hard truths.

The Reality: Is mixing truth with lies creates spiritual poison inside you that can destroy you if left unchecked.

Modern Examples:

Christian yoga and meditation practices.

Combining biblical principles with manifestation techniques.

Adding crystals and energy work to prayer.

Mixing biblical counseling with New Age and New Thought healing modalities.

Biblical Response:

"You cannot drink the cup of the Lord and the cup of demons too; you cannot have a part in both the Lord's table and the table of demons." (1

Corinthians 10:21)

Sixth is the Promise of Secret Knowledge

The Promise: "You will get hidden wisdom beyond what most people know."

The Appeal: Is access to special revelation that makes you part of the spiritually elite.

The Reality: Is gnostic pride that leads away from the simple Truth of the gospel.

Modern Examples:

"Ancient wisdom" that contradicts Scripture.

"Hidden meanings" in biblical texts revealed through occult practices.

"Ascended masters" providing superior spiritual knowledge.

"Quantum revelations" about reality and consciousness.

Biblical Response:

"The secret things belong to the Lord our God, but the things that are revealed belong to us and to our children forever." (Deuteronomy 29:29)

Seventh is Counterfeit Transformation

The Promise: "You can have real change without the cross."

The Appeal: Is personal transformation without death to self.

The Reality: Is behavior modification that leaves the heart unchanged.

Modern Examples:

"Raise your vibration" instead of biblical repentance.

"Mindset shifts" instead of heart transformation.

"Positive thinking" instead of renewing the mind with Scripture.

"Self-love" instead of dying to self and loving God.

Biblical Response:

"If anyone would come after me, let him deny himself and take up his cross and follow me." (Matthew 16:24)

WHY SINCERE PEOPLE FALL INTO DECEPTION

Genuine Spiritual Hunger

God created humans with a spiritual hunger and spiritual needs deep within that only He can satisfy.

When people don't find satisfaction in churches, religions, denominations or traditional Christianity, they seek it elsewhere. With the door wide open, the enemy provides counterfeit spiritual experiences that will temporarily satisfy spiritual hunger.

Unhealed Trauma and Pain

There are many who have experienced trauma in their life—while various and different—all created pain. Painful experiences create vulnerability to anything promising healing. New Age and occult practices often target people in pain. The promise of supernatural healing of physical, mental or emotional needs appeals to those whom traditional medical tactics haven't helped.

Desire for Power and Control

For many, life circumstances often leave them feeling powerless. Spiritual practices promising personal power over circumstances are extremely appealing. Supporting our flesh and mind's desire to be in control rather than surrendering to God.

Cultural Conditioning

Modern culture has normalized Woo and occult practices as "wellness" and "self-improvement." Media, entertainment, and education promote New Age concepts as scientific and progressive. Peer pressure makes spiritual deception seem socially acceptable, as well as what any sane, intelligent, and rational person would do.

Lack of Biblical Foundation

Many Christians lack deep biblical knowledge to recognize deception. Shallow church teaching and lack of self deep-study leaves believers vulnerable to error. Without a solid doctrinal foundation, people can't distinguish truth from lies.

Religious Woundedness

Many who have had negative experiences with churches or church leaders become more open to alternatives. Spiritual abuse makes people reject all religious authority, including biblical truth. The enemy loves using church hurt to drive people into greater deception.

"Those Christians hurt you?"

"Here, try this spiritual alternative that promises to never judge or wound you."

THE PROGRESSION OF SPIRITUAL DECEPTION

First is Initial Attraction

Built into us is a curiosity about spiritual topics—as God put that desire in each of us. And for this very reason, God works tirelessly to bring us to Himself.

But if we don't find Him in a full way, or are traumatized by church hurt, we become open to finding solutions elsewhere.

Many times, we become exposed to the false Woo spiritual through friends, the media, or personal crises. Then, if we experience initial positive encounters with Woo that seem beneficial, it confirms we're on the right track.

With the rationalization that it's "just exploring" or "harmless".

Second is Increasing Involvement

This happens through regular practice of deceptive spiritual techniques—even if in slight movements to begin with. Eventually this grows with users as they become more convinced, perceiving they're gaining spiritual enlightenment.

Ultimately investing in books, courses, and spiritual communities. With increasing experience of supernatural manifestations, which reinforces their decisions and movement. Giving them the reason to defend these practices when questioned by concerned believers.

Third is Identity Integration

As they continue to be deceived further by these experiences, the spiritual practices become central to their personal identity. Making it core to who they are and what they believe. These experiences confirm to them that they have finally found the right path.

Therefore, emboldening them to reject biblical teachings that contradict all these "new beliefs." Eventually, they become practitioners or teachers of these deceptive methods. Causing them to feel spiritually superior to "traditional" Christians.

Fourth is Complete Deception

Ultimately, they come to fully reject biblical Christianity. They become "proud influencers" actively recruiting others into these deceptive practices. Unfortunately, when the enemy has them deeply entrenched in his deceptions, they may begin to experience increasing spiritual oppression and bondage—with potential mental, emotional, and physical consequences.

You might ask why the enemy would do this when he has them "in the palm of his hand."

Why would he oppress and cause pain?

Because his goal was **ALWAYS** to crush every one of us. Hoping we'd never find the Truth and the life God has for us. Read more about his sadistic nature in *THE DAILY STAND*.

Fifth is Crisis and Potential Liberation

The consequences of deception become undeniable. **EVERYONE** who goes down this path will experience spiritual darkness, oppression, and demonic manifestation. Deep crisis will break through the deceptive façade. The enemy's goal is to kill you, and these crises are meant to bring you to that end.

Hopefully, before you give up and die, you'll seize this opportunity for repentance. To return to the biblical Truth that God, the loving Father, has been there waiting for you. And He wants to bring you back to a personal, intimate, deep relationship with Him.

THE SPIRITUAL CONSEQUENCES OF DECEPTION

Immediate Consequences

First: Separation from an authentic, intimate relationship with God.

Second: Opening doors to demonic influence and oppression.

Third: Spiritual confusion and inability to discern truth.

And **Fourth**: Pride that resists correction and accountability to anyone.

Long-term Consequences

First: Progressive hardening of your heart toward biblical truth.

Second: Increasing bondage to spiritual forces.

Third: Damage to relationships with biblical believers and anyone not willing to get on your new "spiritual train" with you.

Fourth: Potential mental, emotional, and physical health problems.

And **Fifth**: Potential death.

Generational Consequences

First: Passing these spiritual deceptions to your children and family.

Second: Creating a spiritual heritage of rebellion against God.

Third: Opening family lines to demonic influence.

Fourth: Breaking the legacy of biblical faith in family for generations to come.

RECOGNIZING SPIRITUAL DECEPTION

Watch for Red Flags in Teaching

First: Claims that contradict clear biblical teaching.

Second: Promises of power, wealth, or control over circumstances.

Third: Appeals to pride or spiritual superiority.

Fourth: Mixing Christian terminology with non-biblical practices.

And **Fifth**: Claiming special revelation beyond Scripture.

Watch for Red Flags in Practice

First: Techniques involving altered states of consciousness.

Second: Practices borrowed from Eastern religions or occult traditions.

Third: Emphasis on supernatural experiences over biblical truth.

Fourth: Requiring secrecy or discouraging questions.

And **Fifth**: Creating dependency on spiritual practitioners or techniques.

Watch for Red Flags in Fruit

First: Increasing spiritual pride and sense of superiority.

Second: Difficulty maintaining relationships with biblical believers.

Third: Defensive reactions when practices are questioned.

Forth: Gradual drift away from biblical truth and fellowship.

And **Fifth**: Unusual spiritual manifestations or oppression.

THE PROTECTION OF BIBLICAL TRUTH

Building Spiritual Immunity

Like physical immunity protects against disease, spiritual immunity protects against deception.

First is Having a Personal Relationship with the Lord

Each one must ask Jesus into his / her life. There's **NO** other way. As stated previously, "Jesus said to him, I am the Way and the Truth and the Life; no one comes to the Father except by (through) Me." (John 14:6)

The Truth of the gospel:

God's Love: "For **God so loved the world** that He gave his only Son, that whoever believes in him shall not perish but have eternal life." (John 3:16)

Sin: "For **ALL have sinned** and fall short of the glory of God." (Romans 3:23)

Consequences of Sin: "For the **Wages of Sin is Death**, but the gift of God is eternal life in Christ Jesus our Lord." (Romans 6:23)

Repentance: "And Peter answered them, **Repent** (change your views and purpose to accept the will of God in your inner selves instead of rejecting it) and be baptized, every one of you, in the name of Jesus Christ **for the forgiveness of** and **release from your sins**; and you shall receive the gift of the Holy Spirit." (Acts 2:38)

Confession and **Belief** lead to **Salvation**: "If you **declare with your mouth**, 'Jesus is Lord,' and **believe in your heart** that God raised him from the dead, you will be saved." (Romans 10:9-10)

Exclusivity of Salvation: "**Salvation is found** in **NO one else**, for there is **NO other name under heaven** given to mankind **by which we must be saved**." (Acts 4:12)

Only by Grace: "For it is **by Grace you have been saved, through faith**—and this is not from yourselves, it is the gift of God—not by works, so that no one can boast." (Ephesians 2:8-9)

Sealed with the Promised Holy Spirit: "In Him you also who have heard the Word of Truth, the glad tidings (Gospel) of your salvation, and have believed in and adhered to and relied on Him, were **stamped** with the **seal of the** [long-promised] **Holy Spirit**. That [Spirit] is the **Guarantee of our inheritance** [the firstfruits, the pledge and foretaste, the down payment on our heritage], in anticipation of its full redemption and our acquiring [complete] possession of it — to the praise of His glory." (Ephesians 1:13-14)

So, if you haven't met the Lord already, here's a simple prayer for you:

"Jesus, I know I am a sinner, and I ask that you forgive me. I repent (I turn away from my sin). I believe that you died on the cross for my sins and that God raised you from the dead. Jesus, I believe that you are Lord and Savior! I ask that you come into my life and my heart. Help me grow in my relationship with you. Thank You! Amen."

Second is Regular Study of Scripture

Knowing God's Word prevents accepting counterfeits. You must study God's Word deeply. Not taking any teacher, preacher, minister, pastor, priest or leader's word for it. [Including me.]

"Be diligent to present yourself approved to God as a workman who does not need to be ashamed, who correctly and accurately handles the word of truth." (2 Timothy 2:15)

"Now these [Bereans] were better disposed and more noble than those in Thessalonica, for they were entirely ready and accepted and welcomed the message [concerning the attainment through Christ of eternal salvation in the kingdom of God] with inclination of mind and eagerness, searching and examining the Scriptures daily to see if these things were so. (Acts 17:11)

"The secret things belong unto the Lord our God, but the things which are revealed belong to us and to our children forever, that we may do all of the words of this law." (Deuteronomy 29:29)

Third is THE PEACE

I will not reiterate what I previously said about **THE PEACE**. If you didn't catch the depth and need, please go back to read in full.

In short, I'll simply restate Philippians 4:7: "And **THE PEACE** of God, which transcends all understanding and comprehension, will guard your hearts and your minds in Christ Jesus."

Fourth is Biblical Fellowship

Staying in fellowship with mature believers provides protection.

"For wherever two or three are gathered (drawn together as My followers) in (into) My name, there I AM in the midst of them." (Matthew 18:20)

"Not forsaking or neglecting to assemble together [as believers], as is the habit of some people, but admonishing (warning, urging, and encouraging) one another, and all the more faithfully as you see the day approaching." (Hebrews 10:25)

Fifth is Prayer and Worship

An intimate relationship with God is the ONLY thing that satisfies spiritual hunger.

Prayer is NOT about clasped hands or being on your knees for hours. Prayer is simple communication with God, the Father. It isn't limited to times or locations. It should be a daily part of our lives. From the time we wake until the time we fall asleep—talking/communicating with Papa God is a privilege—not a duty.

When we learn that He wants to talk to us more than we want to talk to Him, it can become transforming.

Worship is NOT about what songs you sing nor how great the song leader or worship team is. It's about the depth of love and song that issues from your innermost being, then flows from you to God. It's NOT the words nor the tune—it's about the Holy Spirit flowing through you to Him.

Learn more about these subjects in both *THE DAILY STAND* and *SET THE CAPTIVES FREE*.

Sixth is Humble Teachability

Acknowledging "we only know in part" prevents pride. We MUST remain teachable—before God and [humbled] believers. I teach this in depth in *SET THE CAPTIVES FREE*.

If you haven't read my first two books, please do so. There are many areas covered in them you'll need to survive the many deceptions all around us.

Seventh is Discernment Training

You MUST learn to test all spiritual claims against Scripture. As stated previously in 1 John 4:1-3,

"Beloved, **do not put faith in every spirit**, but **prove (test) the spirits** to **discover** whether they proceed from God; for many false prophets have gone forth into the world. By this you may know (perceive and recognize) the Spirit of God: every spirit which acknowledges and confesses [the fact] that Jesus Christ (the Messiah) [actually] has become man and has come in the flesh is of God [has God for its source]; And **every spirit which does not acknowledge** and **confess that Jesus Christ** has come in the flesh [but would annul, destroy, sever, disunite Him] **is not of God** [does not proceed from Him]. This [nonconfession] is the [spirit] of the antichrist, [of] which you heard that it was coming, and now it is already in the world."

This training, backed by knowing Scripture in depth [including the original Greek and Hebrew] along with **THE PEACE** will guide you and guard your hearts and minds.

THE WISE SERPENT PRINCIPLE

Jesus told us to be "Wise as serpents and innocent as doves." (Matthew 10:16)

We must understand the enemy's tactics without participating in them.

We need to recognize deception without being deceived by it.

We must protect ourselves and others through knowledge and discernment.

And we must maintain purity [by yielding to the Holy Spirit] while engaging a corrupted spiritual environment.

KEY POINTS TO REMEMBER

First: Spiritual deception always appears beneficial and appealing.

Second: All deception follows the Genesis pattern of questioning God's authority.

Third: The "common pillars" support most spiritual deceptions.

Fourth: Sincere people fall into deception through unmet needs, vulnerabilities, abuses, and trauma.

And **Fifth**: Biblical truth provides protection against all forms of deception.

You MUST understand the

BATTLEFIELD to win.

CHAPTER EIGHT

TYPES OF DECEPTIONS

FOUNDATIONAL DECEPTIONS

The Foundation of All Spiritual Error: Rejecting God's Authority While Seeking Spiritual Experience

So here's the key mistake:

IGNORING GOD'S AUTHORITY WHILE exploring spirituality.

Woo. Lies. New Age. Occult practices. ALL of it. Every single deceptive spiritual pathway you'll encounter traces back to this ONE foundational error—the basis for EVERY false belief system since the Garden of Eden.

It creates a false spiritual framework that appears satisfying while leading people away from an authentic relationship with God.

Understanding this foundational error is crucial because it represents the core behind ALL the lies that Satan uses to deceive sincere spiritual seekers. Once people accept this foundation, they become vulnerable to increasingly dangerous spiritual practices.

I mean, why bother with a relationship with the Creator of the Universe when you can just manifest your own reality, right? Who needs the God who spoke everything into existence when you've got vision boards and positive affirmations?

I mean, obviously, YOUR thoughts are powerful enough to reshape the cosmos.

Makes total sense.

No duh!

"SPIRITUALITY" WITHOUT BIBLICAL FOUNDATION

The Core Deception Claims

Here's what they're selling you:

You can have a personal connection to divine forces without biblical constraints. All spiritual paths are identical, leading to the same destination. Your individual spiritual experience is more important than biblical doctrine. And you can create your own spiritual belief system.

The Hidden Reality:

This represents rebellion against God's authority disguised as simple spiritual seeking to "find God." It allows people to feel spiritual while rejecting the moral accountability and surrender an authentic relationship with God requires.

Yeah, because the God who created you, died for you, and wants an actual relationship with you is just too demanding. Much better to cherry-pick from a spiritual buffet—a little Buddhism here, some crystals there, maybe a dash of astrology, and top it off with whatever makes you feel good.

Spiritual junk food.

Tastes great going down.

Only destroys you from the inside.

So, not a problem, right?

Why This Deception Appeals

This deception appeals to the Flesh:

When it offers a spiritual experience without moral demands. Allowing cherry-picking of appealing spiritual concepts to suit your feelings and needs. As well as providing a sense of spiritual superiority over "religious" people. And it eliminates any accountability to divine authority.

This deception appeals to human pride:

When it makes the individual the ultimate spiritual authority. It allows feeling "more evolved" than traditional believers. It provides a basis for judging others as "less enlightened". And it creates the illusion of spiritual sophistication.

This deception appeals to wounded hearts:

When it offers spiritual healing without dealing with sin. It provides an alternative for those hurt or abused by churches and/or leaders. It promises unquestioned acceptance without repentance. It appeals to those who reject the organized church—and to those who have been wounded by it;

And I get it. I really do.

Have you ever been hurt by a church? By religious leaders? By people who claimed to represent God but acted nothing like Him?

Join the club. There are a LOT of us.

But here's the thing—running from religious abuse straight into Satan's arms isn't exactly an upgrade. It's like escaping a bad restaurant and then diving into a dumpster for dinner. Sure, you're out of the restaurant, but...

COMMON EXPRESSIONS

"Spiritual But Not Religious"

This rejects the organized church while maintaining spiritual beliefs. It often combines elements from multiple religious traditions and sources. It emphasizes personal spiritual experience over the revealed Truth of God as the more important indicator of true spirituality. It creates an individual spiritual framework based on your own personal preferences.

In other words: "I'll be my own god, thank you very much."

"All Paths Lead to God"

This claims all religions teach the same basic truth. Absolutely rejecting Jesus as the exclusive path to salvation. It promotes religious universalism and tolerance of all spiritual paths. And denies the uniqueness of biblical revelation.

Sure. All paths lead to God. That's why Jesus said, "I am THE Way, THE Truth, and THE Life. NO ONE comes to the Father EXCEPT through Me." (John 14:6)

We're pretty sure we know He must've meant ALL the paths lead to Him. Because 'THE Way' and 'NO ONE except through Me' really scream 'multiple options available.'

Come on, people.

"Inner Divine Wisdom"

This teaches that complete divine wisdom exists within every person. Promoting meditation and contemplative practices as the key to accessing this wisdom. This often leads to spirit contact with the wrong sources disguised as "inner guidance." And rejects the notion of external biblical authority in favor of internal "knowing."

Translation: Trust your gut over God's Word.

Because that's worked out so well throughout human history.

"Create Your Own Spiritual Path"

This encourages individuals to design personal spiritual systems—which can grow dynamically—based on their continued spiritual enlightenment. It combines Christian terminology with non-biblical practices to make it palatable to the masses who seek to do the same. Many times including elements of Eastern mysticism, New Age concepts, and occult practices. All of this leads to spiritual confusion and deception.

THE REAL TRUTH: THERE'S ONLY ONE WAY TO REACH GOD

As mentioned previously from John 14:6, "Jesus said to him, 'I am THE Way, and THE Truth, and THE Life. NO ONE comes to the Father except through me'."

This verse completely contradicts the universalist teaching that all spiritual paths lead to God. Jesus made the exclusive claim to be the **ONLY** way to an authentic relationship with God, the Father.

Period.

Deal with it.

The Authority of Scripture

"All Scripture is God-breathed (given by His inspiration) and profitable for instruction, for reproof and conviction of sin, for correction of error and discipline in obedience, [and] for training in righteousness (in holy living, in conformity to God's will in thought, purpose, and action)." (2 Timothy 3:16)

God has revealed His Truth through His written Word, **NOT** through individual spiritual experiences or human wisdom. Scripture provides the standard for evaluating **ALL** spiritual claims.

I know, I know. "But Tom, the Bible was written by men! It's been translated so many times! It's outdated!"

Right. So instead, you'll trust the New Age blogger who channels "Ascended Master Joan eRamirez" from their apartment in Portland. Or the guy selling you a $500 crystal healing kit. Or the TikTok spiritualist with the ring light and the zodiac tapestry.

Ah, now I understand.

Much more reliable sources.

The Deception of Human Wisdom

"Where is the wise man (the philosopher)? Where is the scribe (the scholar)? Where is the investigator (the logician, the debater) of this present time and age? Has not God shown up the nonsense and the folly of this world's wisdom?" (1 Corinthians 1:20)

Human spiritual wisdom apart from God's revelation **ALWAYS** leads to deception and error. True spiritual wisdom comes directly from God through His Word, by His Spirit, and confirmed by His Perfect PEACE.

The Deception of the False Spiritual

The cynical goal of the god of this world and his diverse offerings of the false spiritual is not just to deceive **ALL** of mankind by Woo. Instead, his goal is to get **ALL** of mankind to walk in rebellion to the One and Only, True God—whom he hates. Then, in the end, he'll destroy **EVERYONE** who followed him, dragging them to hell along with him and his demon spirits—where he knows they're going.

"For rebellion is as the sin of divination and witchcraft; and arrogance and stubbornness are like the evil of iniquity, idolatry, and teraphim (household good luck images). Because you have rejected the word of the Lord, He also has rejected you." (1 Samuel 15:23)

"In which at one time you [habitually] walked. You were following the course and fashion of this world [were under the sway of the tendency of this present age], following the prince of the power of the air [the god of this world]. [You were obedient to and under the control of] the [demon] spirit(s) that still constantly work in the sons of disobedience [the careless, the rebellious, and the unbelieving, who go against the purposes of God]." (Ephesians 2:2)

"And the devil who deceived them was thrown into the lake of fire and brimstone, where the beast and the false prophet are also; and they will be tormented day and night forever and ever." (Revelation 20:10)

"And if anyone's name was not found written in the book of life, he was thrown into the lake of fire." (Revelation 20:15)

These verses are included here not to preach hellfire and brimstone as some do. Instead, they're here as a warning of the serious consequences that await those who choose **NOT** to follow the Lord.

The Path to Freedom

First, we need to acknowledge that rejecting biblical authority while seeking spiritual experience is **rebellion** against God.

Second, we must recognize that personal spiritual experiences must be tested against Scripture.

Third, we need to admit that human wisdom is insufficient for understanding spiritual Truth.

Then lastly, we need to accept that the Bible's exclusive claims about Truth are necessary for authentic spirituality.

MANIFESTATION AND REALITY MANIPULATION

The Core Deception of both these commonly accepted functions is false. Both claim humans have divine power to create their own reality through thoughts and intentions. They claim the universe responds to human desires and beliefs. They claim you can attract whatever you want through spiritual techniques. Also claiming that reality is malleable and subject to human consciousness.

The Hidden Reality is that these things represent the ultimate expression of human pride. The belief that humans can function as gods—controlling and creating reality through spiritual manipulation. It's modern witchcraft disguised as positive thinking and spiritual empowerment.

So let me get this straight. You think your thoughts can reshape reality?

Your brain—the same brain that forgets where you put your car keys and convinces you that texting your ex at 2 AM is a good idea—is somehow powerful enough to bend the fabric of the universe to your will?

Okay then.

The Historical Roots are deeply embedded in ancient occult practices: Egyptian and Babylonian magic rituals. Hermetic philosophy: "As above, so below." Gnostic teachings about human divinity. And witchcraft and sorcery throughout history.

It's just a **New Modern Repackaging** of the "New Thought" movement (from the 19th century), positive thinking philosophy, the human potential movement, and Quantum mysticism and consciousness studies.

Common Manifestation Teachings

Again, the "Law of Attraction" teaching "Like attracts like." Stating positive thoughts attract positive outcomes; and negative thoughts attract negative outcomes. But the reality is, this makes individuals responsible for all circumstances, including tragedies and suffering. It also attempts to manipulate spiritual forces for personal gain.

"Many plans are in a man's mind, but it is [only] the Lord's purpose for him that will stand." (Proverbs 19:21)

So when a child gets cancer, that's because they were thinking negatively?

When someone loses their job in a recession, they attracted it?

Tell that to Job. Tell that to Paul in prison. Tell that to Jesus on the cross.

I guess they just weren't thinking positively enough while being tortured for their faith.

"Visualization and Affirmations"

These philosophies teach that repeatedly visualizing desired outcomes with affirming positive statements will manifest those desires in reality. This form of meditation and thought opens the mind to spiritual influence when attempting to control circumstances through mental techniques. Unfortunately, the Lord will not honor such practices—yet the god of this world will. Regrettably, those who practice such have just opened themselves to the wrong spirits; which will have negative consequences.

Understand that God is not against visions. He said in Acts 2:17, "In the last days, God says, 'I will pour out my Spirit on all people. Your sons and daughters will prophesy, your young men will see visions, and your old men will dream dreams."

The distinct difference between these two types of visions is when walking with the True and Living God, **He gives** visions to His people, versus in "visualization" people are creating spiritual visions in their minds for themselves. No human can create spiritual visions. In striving to achieve this by opening to the wrong spiritual realm, the wrong spirits will answer them.

So let me understand this: You're going to sit in a quiet room, empty your mind, and visualize yourself driving a new BMW.

And you think God is going to honor that?

Or maybe—just maybe—you've opened up a spiritual portal and something else is answering. Something that doesn't have your best interest at heart but is very happy to start a relationship with you.

Hard to believe, but the devil doesn't have your best interest at heart.

NO, DUH!

"Thus says the Lord: 'Cursed [with great evil] is the one who trusts and relies in mankind and makes mere flesh his strength, whose heart turns away from and departs from the Lord... Blessed is the one who believes in, trusts in, and relies on the Lord, and whose hope and confidence is the

Lord [alone].'" (Jeremiah 17:5-7)

"Gratitude and Abundance Mindset"

These philosophies teach by feeling grateful for what you want before you receive it, you will attract it into your life. While gratitude is biblical, unfortunately, using it as a technique to "manipulate the universe" to create your desired outcomes will not work. Regrettably again, the Lord will not honor such practices—yet the god of this world will. Meaning your good intentions become another opening for spiritual evil.

"Trust in the Lord with all your heart and lean not on your own understanding; in all your ways submit to him, and he will make your paths straight." (Proverbs 3:5-6)

What are the Spiritual Dangers in doing this?

First: Pride in believing you can control reality.

Second: Frustration and self-blame when all these manifestations "fail."

Third: Opening to demonic influence through meditation and visualization.

Fourth: Replacing prayer and submission to God with spiritual manipulation.

Fifth: Progressive hardening against biblical truth about God's sovereignty.

Sixth: Increasing involvement in occult and spirit practices and contact.

Seventh: Mental and emotional instability from trying to control uncontrollable circumstances.

Eighth: Eventual spiritual oppression and demonic influence.

Other Dangers

First: Judging others for "negative thinking" when they experience difficulties.

Second: Blaming victims or others for attracting negative circumstances.

Third: Creating superficial relationships with other like-minded people based on "positive energy".

Fourth: Isolating from biblical believers who would challenge manifestation practices.

Fifth: Judging believers for not being as "in tune" with the universe as they've become.

The Alternative: Prayer and Surrender

Let's look at biblical prayer versus manifestation:

Prayer submits all our desires to God's will and timing. While manifestation demands specific outcomes according to the human will. Prayer acknowledges God's sovereignty over all circumstances. While manifestation claims human power to control circumstances. Prayer brings **THE PEACE** through surrender and trust in the Holy Spirit. While manifestation creates anxiety through responsibility for outcomes.

"And this is the **Confidence** (the assurance, the privilege of boldness) which **we have in Him**: that if we ask anything **According to His will (in agreement with His own plan**), He listens to and hears us. And if (since) we [positively] know that He listens to us in whatever we ask, we also know [with settled and absolute knowledge] that we will have the requests made of Him." (1 John 5:14-15)

True prayer involves aligning our desires with God's will.

Then trusting in His perfect timing and methods. Finding **His PEACE** in His sovereign love despite outcomes. And accepting His answers even when different from our requests—trusting that His reasons are greater than our knowledge—and He always knows what's best for us.

"For I know the plans I have for you, declares the Lord, plans to prosper you and not to harm you, plans to give you hope and a future." (Jeremiah 29:11)

"For my thoughts are not your thoughts, neither are your ways my ways, declares the Lord. As the heavens are higher than the earth, so are my ways higher than your ways and my thoughts than your thoughts." (Isaiah 55:8-9)

"And we know that in all things God works for the good of those who love him, who have been called according to his purpose." (Romans 8:28)

The bottom line:

You can spend your life trying to manipulate the universe with your thoughts, chasing manifestation techniques, and opening yourself up to spiritual forces that don't have your best interests at heart.

Or you can surrender to the God who actually created you, actually loves you, actually died for you, and actually has a plan for your life that's better than anything you could manifest in a vision board session.

Your choice.

Choose wisely.

ENERGY AND CONSCIOUSNESS DECEPTIONS

Seeking Power Apart from the ONLY Source

The appeal of Spiritual Power is that we as human beings can somehow obtain it and operate as God does. Woo and **ALL** false spiritual sources tell you that you can have that for yourself—but that's just part of the masquerade.

Isn't that the same delusion that Satan / Lucifer operated under that caused him to be kicked out of Heaven? Believing he could be equal to God?

ABSOLUTELY!

Satan was God's most powerful cherub, archangel and creation, who thought he was greater than God, his creator, and could challenge God, so God cast him to the earth.

"How you have fallen from Heaven, morning star, son of the dawn! You have been cast down to the earth, you who once laid low the nations! You said in your heart, 'I will ascend to the heavens; I will raise my throne above the stars of God; I will sit enthroned on the mount of assembly, on the utmost heights of Mount Zaphon. I will ascend above the tops of the clouds; I will make myself like the Most High.' But you are brought down to the realm of the dead, to the depths of the pit." (Isaiah 14:12–15)

"You were in Eden, the garden of God; every precious stone adorned you...your settings and mountings were made of gold; on the day you were created they were prepared. You were anointed as a guardian cherub, for so I ordained you. You were on the holy mount of God; you walked among the fiery stones. You were blameless in your ways from the day you were created. Until wickedness was found in you. Through your widespread trade you were filled with violence, and you sinned. So, I drove you in disgrace from the mount of God, and I expelled you, guardian cherub, from among the fiery stones. Your heart became proud on account of your beauty, and you corrupted your wisdom because of your splendor. So, I threw you to the earth; I made a spectacle of you before kings." (Ezekiel 28:13–17)

So the MOST powerful being in the universe ever created, thought he could be like God, and it got him kicked out of Heaven; with the promise to be thrown into a lake of fire for eternity.

And you think you're better, smarter and more capable by tapping into "universal energy" and becoming godlike?

Good luck with that.

To the opposite, we were created to walk with the True and Living God, who has **ALL** True Spiritual Power. Not that we have any such power in us, but we can experience it alongside Him, when we are in connection with and in submission to Him. I explain this in great detail in *THE DAILY STAND*.

In the masquerade, energy and consciousness deceptions promise the True Spiritual Power they cannot give—while disconnecting people from the One and Only True Source—leading them to seek power from created forces rather than the Creator.

These deceptions are particularly dangerous because they often produce real "supernatural experiences" and apparent results—making them seem legitimate and beneficial. However, the power accessed through these practices comes from demonic sources and leads to increasing spiritual bondage.

ENERGY MANIPULATION PRACTICES

"Tapping into Universal Energy"

Claiming the universe contains unlimited spiritual energy available to humans. This energy is neutral and can be accessed through meditation and spiritual techniques. Humans can learn to manipulate this energy for healing, empowerment, and manifestation. Different cultures have identified this energy as "chi" (Chinese), "prana" (Hindu), and "ki" (Japanese).

The truth is, there are no neutral spiritual forces. All spiritual power comes from either God or demonic sources. "Universal energy" practices involve contact with familiar spirits presenting themselves as impersonal forces.

Some common practices discussed previously are Reiki, Energy Healing, Chakra Work, Qi Gong, Tai Chi, Crystal Healing, and Acupuncture.

Once again, we need to understand that God is the **ONLY** source of **ALL** legitimate power and healing. Seeking power from other sources opens doors to demonic influence—which the god of this world is more than happy to fill—ALWAYS.

"And my God will supply every need of yours according to his riches in glory in Christ Jesus." (Philippians 4:19)

"But Tom, my Reiki practitioner is so nice! And I felt something! It must be from God!"

Yeah, Satan was "nice" to Eve too. He seemed very helpful. He just wanted her to have more knowledge and to be more like God.

How'd that work out?

"Energetic Healing and Empowerment"

Claiming humans can become channels for healing energy. This channeled energy can heal physical, emotional, and spiritual problems. With the "laying on of hands" [which differs from how the Bible teaches], visualization, and invoking spiritual entities. Promoting that traditional medicine is inferior to energy healing.

The reality is, energy healing practices involve contacting the wrong spiritual forces. Invoking entities or "ascended masters" for power. Championing visualization to create altered states of consciousness, opening their minds to spiritual influence. Endorsing transference where actual spiritual forces move between practitioner and client. Creating dependency and reliance on practitioners channeling spirits rather than God.

Biblical healing involves: Prayer in Jesus' name rather than allowing the wrong spirits to channel through energy manipulation. Depending on God's sovereignty rather than human techniques combined with demon forces. Walking in faith in Christ rather than allowing the wrong spirits to transfer their spiritual energy. Remaining in a relationship with God in His **Perfect PEACE**.

If you haven't read *THE DAILY STAND*, you really need to do that to understand what channeling and transference by these seemingly harmless spiritual engagements will do to **ALL** who practice such.

CONSCIOUSNESS EXPANSION DECEPTIONS

"Higher Consciousness and Enlightenment"

Claiming human consciousness can evolve beyond normal awareness. Through meditation and spiritual practices, people can achieve "enlightenment." Higher consciousness provides access to universal knowledge and divine wisdom. And enlightened individuals transcend ordinary human limitations.

These teachings promote the lie that humans can achieve godlike consciousness through self-effort. Leading to spiritual pride; involving contact with deceiving spirits providing counterfeit wisdom and experiences.

Common practices are Transcendental Meditation, Mindfulness Meditation, Breathwork, Sensory Deprivation, and Plant Medicine.

"But I felt so peaceful! So connected! So enlightened!"

Yeah, that's how deception works.

It feels good.

It seems right.

It appears beneficial.

You know what else feels good? That first drink for an alcoholic. That first hit for an addict. That first taste for someone developing an eating disorder.

Feelings aren't truth. They're just feelings. And demons are very good at creating feelings.

Consciousness expansion appeals to human pride by promising access to "hidden knowledge." Creating feelings of spiritual superiority. Offering an escape from human limitations. Providing a sense of personal spiritual achievement.

True spiritual wisdom comes from a personal, living relationship with the One True God, not from consciousness expansion techniques. Attempting to achieve divine consciousness through human effort represents the original sin of wanting to "be like God."

"Quantum Consciousness and Reality Creation"

Misusing quantum physics to suggest consciousness can create reality. Claiming access to "quantum fields" to manifest desired outcomes. Changing consciousness changes physical reality. Promoting that scientific discoveries support these spiritual practices.

Quantum mysticism misrepresents legitimate science, taking quantum principles out of context from the subatomic to the macroscale. Confusing observation with consciousness in quantum mechanics. Ignoring the role of measurement apparatus in quantum experiments. Making unsupported leaps from physics to metaphysics.

Leading to Reality Dissociation—believing you can alter fundamental reality. Causing mental instability and confusion about reality. Creating Spiritual Deception, opening practitioners to entities claiming to be "quantum guides." Causing pride and delusion—believing you have godlike power over reality.

God is the Creator and sustainer of reality. While we were created in His image, we cannot alter reality through consciousness manipulation.

Here's what you need to understand:

ALL of these practices—energy manipulation, consciousness expansion, quantum mysticism—they all have one thing in common.

They promise you can be like God without actually submitting to God.

That's the same lie Satan has been selling since Eden.

And it's still a lie.

ANCIENT WISDOM AND OCCULT PRACTICES

These are Recycled Paganism in Modern Packaging

What is the appeal of "Ancient Wisdom"?

Modern spiritual seekers believe that older spiritual practices contain superior wisdom lost by Christianity. Appeal to "ancient wisdom" represents one of Satan's most effective strategies—the repackaging of age-old occult practices in **NEW** modern forms.

These "ancient wisdom" teachings represent the same spiritual deceptions that God's people have been warned against throughout Scripture. They're not superior spiritual insights—they're recycled paganism designed to lead people away from biblical truth.

"But Tom, it's been around for THOUSANDS of years! It must have some truth to it!"

You know what else has been around for thousands of years? Murder. Adultery. Theft. Idolatry.

Age doesn't equal truth.

It just means Satan's been using this particular lie for a really long time.

If anything, that should make you more suspicious, not less.

The "Ancient Wisdom" Deception

Claims pre-Christian spiritual practices contain superior wisdom from the ages. Believing ancient civilizations had spiritual knowledge modern Christianity has lost. Stating Indigenous and Eastern spiritual traditions are more authentic. Urging theological authorities have hidden this secret wisdom from ordinary people so they can use it to control them.

All "ancient wisdom" represents the same occult practices condemned in Scripture. These practices led ancient civilizations into spiritual darkness and moral corruption.

"Secret knowledge" claims have always been tools of spiritual deception.

"See to it that **no one takes you captive** by **philosophy** and **empty deceit**, according to **human tradition**, according to the **elemental spirits of the world**, and not according to Christ." (Colossians 2:8)

Common "Ancient Wisdom" Practices

Eastern Mysticism, like Hindu and Buddhist practices, have been adapted for Western consumption. Such as yoga—which was originally designed for union with Hindu deities. While yoga is promoted as simply "great exercise", the participants unknowingly become open to the spiritual forces behind it. The same with meditation, which involves emptying the mind or invoking spiritual entities, has become widely adapted in many forms. Along with using mantras—that induce altered states and spirit contact.

Using Chakras, denoting the Hindu energy system. Promoting Karma and Reincarnation belief systems that deny biblical salvation.

These practices have been repackaged and presented as physical exercise, stress relief, mental health and wellness techniques. Championing cultural appreciation and tolerance. Lobbying they provide scientific and psychological benefits.

ALL these practices **RETAIN** their spiritual components and open practitioners to spiritual deception and confusion. Creating contact with Hindu, Buddhist, and other spiritual entities. Building a gradual adoption of Eastern worldviews that contradict Scripture. Enhancing the movement away from biblical Christianity.

Indigenous Shamanism

Native and Tribal Spiritual practices, such as Shamanic Journeying — entering altered states to contact spirit guides. Contacting Animal Spirits to seek guidance from animal spirit entities. Utilizes Plant Medicine's psychoactive substances for spiritual experiences. Sweat Lodges and Vision Quests ritual practices for spiritual transformation. And Sacred Geometry and Earth Energy — believing spiritual powers are found at certain locations.

Shamanic practices appeal to people seeking a connection with nature and environmental concerns. Promises an authentic spiritual experience. Advocates healing of trauma and emotional wounds. Promotes an enlightened sense of spiritual adventure and power.

EVERY Shamanic practice involves direct contact with familiar spirits posing as helpful guides. Altering the consciousness of the practitioners—opening them to demonic influence. Including ritual involvement—which creates spiritual bondage and obligation. This is a progressive deception—leading deeper into occult involvement.

Western Occult Traditions

European and American Occult practices such as Wicca and Modern Witchcraft involve the worship of nature deities and spell casting. Including ceremonial magic rituals for invoking spiritual entities. Using divination by Tarot cards, astrology, crystal balls, and other fortune-telling methods to obtain perceived results. Championing spiritualism to contact the spirits of the dead. Advocating Alchemy and Hermeticism—which are ancient chemical and philosophical occult systems.

The modern repackaging presents these practices as feminist spirituality and goddess worship; historical and cultural study; psychological tools and self-help techniques; as well as entertainment and harmless fun.

The truth is that **ALL** Western occult practices involve demon worship disguised as nature or goddess spirituality. Championing spell-casting, attempting to manipulate reality through spiritual forces. With divination, seeking information from demons about the future. Using necromancy disguised as communication with deceased loved ones.

The Neurodivergence and Intuitive Coaching Deception

Claiming spiritual neurodivergence and certain neurological differences indicate "special" spiritual gifts. Stating ADHD, autism, and other conditions are actually signs of "spiritual sensitivity." Neurodivergent individuals are naturally more "intuitive" and spiritually gifted. Believing traditional therapy is inferior to spiritual approaches for neurodivergent people.

Spiritualizing mental health conditions rather than addressing them appropriately. Creating a false identity based on neurological differences rather than a relationship with God. Leading to the neglect of proper medical and therapeutic care. Opening the door to spiritual deception through "intuitive" guidance.

"Intuitive Coaching" and Spiritual Guidance

Claiming these coaches receive supernatural guidance for their clients. Involving divination techniques disguised as "intuition." Including energy healing, psychic readings, and spirit contact. Promising spiritual insights and life direction through human practitioners.

The Problem is it bypasses Scripture as the source of guidance and wisdom. Creating a dependency on human practitioners rather than God. Involving divination that's forbidden in Scripture. Replacing biblical counseling with occult practices.

True guidance comes from God's Word as the primary source of direction. Including prayer and a relationship with God through Jesus Christ, and most importantly, with the Holy Spirit's inner witness confirmed by **THE PEACE**.

THE BOTTOM LINE

Every deception we've covered—foundational errors, manifestation, energy manipulation, consciousness expansion, ancient wisdom, occult practices—they all share the same spiritual DNA.

They all promise spiritual power and experience apart from submission to the One True God.

They all dress up rebellion as enlightenment.

They all make the creature the center instead of the Creator.

And they all lead to the same destination: spiritual bondage, demonic influence, and separation from the God who actually loves you and actually died for you.

The path to freedom is NOT found in ANY of these practices.

It's found in a relationship with Jesus Christ, submission to God's Word, and walking in the power of the Holy Spirit.

That's it. That's the only path.

EVERYTHING ELSE IS JUST A MASQUERADE.

CHAPTER NINE

DIRECT LINE INTO THE SPIRIT REALM

W E **ALL** CRAVE CONNECTION to the spiritual realm—deeply, fully, intimately. Papa God, the Father, created us that way on purpose. He put that desire in us so **ALL** souls would come to Him and know Him intimately. Yet He limited access to the **TRUE** spiritual realm with **ONLY** one way to reach Him—through His Son, Jesus, and the cross.

As mentioned previously from John 14:6, "Jesus said to him, I am THE Way and THE Truth and THE Life; NO one comes to the Father except by (through) Me."

And we're told in Matthew 7:13-14,

"**Enter through the narrow gate**; for the gate is wide and the way is broad that leads to destruction, and there are many who enter through it. For the **gate is small** and the **way is narrow** that leads to life, and **there are few** who find it."

But who wants a narrow gate when there's a whole spiritual buffet out there, right?

Tarot cards. Mediums. Psychics. Channelers. Spirit guides. Ascended masters. Your "higher self." The universe. Crystals. Energy healers. Shamans. Ayahuasca ceremonies. Past life regression. Akashic records.

So many options!

So many doorways!

So many ways to tap into the spiritual realm and feel connected.

Just one tiny problem.

They're ALL connected to the wrong side.

JUST BECAUSE...

Just because you can connect to the spirit realm is never enough.

Just because you hear from the spirit realm doesn't mean it's from the right source.

Just because it feels good doesn't mean it is good.

Just because it seems helpful doesn't mean it's not harmful.

Just because it appears to be light doesn't mean it's not darkness in disguise.

"The way is broad that leads to destruction."

"But Tom, I had this amazing spiritual experience! I felt so at peace! I received such profound guidance! It couldn't possibly be from the enemy—it was too beautiful!"

Yeah, that's kind of the point.

If the enemy showed up looking like the enemy, nobody would fall for it. If demons announced themselves as demons, if deception looked like deception, if the trap looked like a trap—nobody would walk into it.

The enemy has been perfecting his disguises for thousands of years. He's had a lot of practice.

And you think your "discernment" is going to outsmart him?

Good luck with that.

CONNECTING TO THE SPIRITUAL REALM

The desire to connect to the spiritual realm is hardwired into us. It's not wrong. It's not a flaw. Papa God designed us this way.

The spiritual realm is real. Very Real.

It confirms there's a realm above us.

It creates a desire to connect more.

It feels good.

It feels powerful.

It makes you feel special.

This is why it's an easy deception for many to fall into.

The Truth:

There's the good side of the spiritual realm, which we can experience with One and Only, True God on a daily, moment-by-moment basis. This relationship is worth digging through all the counterfeits to find the **ONLY** thing that will truly fulfill and satisfy your need for the spiritual realm. It's worth more than all the riches in the world.

Walking with the True and Living God—experiencing His Presence, hearing His voice, feeling His love, knowing His guidance—this is what your soul was created for.

Everything else is a counterfeit. A knockoff. A cheap imitation that promises fulfillment but delivers bondage.

The Counterfeits:

There's a dark side of the spiritual realm we can experience with the god of this world and his demon forces. **ALL** flaunted in front of us in many forms. **ALL** disguised to lead us astray from the **ONLY** one true answer. **ALL** wearing masks promoting this **Great Evil Masquerade** in life.

The Counterfeits include:

Divination — Tarot cards, palm reading, astrology, tea leaves, crystal balls, runes, I Ching, pendulums. All of these seek information about the future or hidden knowledge from spiritual sources other than God. They're forbidden in Scripture for a reason—they open direct lines to demonic spirits.

Mediums and Channelers — People who claim to communicate with the dead or channel spiritual entities. What they're actually doing is communicating with familiar spirits—demons who masquerade as deceased loved ones or "ascended beings." The dead don't come back. But demons are more than happy to play the role.

Psychics and Clairvoyants — Those claiming supernatural knowledge or insight. The power is real—it just doesn't come from God. It comes from demonic sources that provide accurate information to establish trust, then use that trust to lead people deeper into deception.

Spirit Guides and Ascended Masters — Supposed spiritual beings that offer guidance and wisdom. In reality, these are demonic entities presenting themselves as helpful guides. They offer "wisdom" that draws people away from biblical truth and deeper into spiritual bondage.

Plant Medicine Ceremonies — Ayahuasca, psilocybin, peyote, and other psychedelics used for "spiritual awakening." These substances alter consciousness and open direct portals to the demonic realm. The "entities" encountered are not benevolent teachers—they're demons taking advantage of a chemically-induced open door.

Shamanic Journeying — Entering altered states to contact spirit guides and receive spiritual wisdom. This is direct spirit contact with demonic entities, no matter how "ancient" or "indigenous" the practice.

Energy Healing and Reiki — Channeling "universal energy" for healing. As we discussed in the previous chapter, there is no neutral spiritual energy. What's being channeled is demonic power, and both the practitioner and the client are opening themselves to demonic influence.

"But Tom, my psychic was so accurate! She knew things nobody could have known!"

Of course she did. Demons have been observing humanity for thousands of years. They know your family history. They were there when things happened. They know the secrets. They know the details.

The accuracy isn't proof that it's from God. The accuracy is the bait.

You know what else is accurate? A fishhook covered with the perfect lure. The fish thinks it's getting a meal. Instead, it gets caught.

Same principle. Different pond.

DECEIVED THINKING

Is it possible that good, sincere Christian believers can be deceived into thinking they're hearing from God, yet not?

YES.

Rightly so, you might ask:

"Why?"

"How?"

"Wouldn't God protect His people from such?"

Fair questions. Important questions. Let me address them.

Why Sincere Believers Get Deceived

First: Because they don't know what they don't know. Many believers have never been taught about the tactics of the enemy. They've never been warned about counterfeit spiritual experiences. They assume that if something feels spiritual and seems positive, it must be from God.

Second: Because they're not deeply rooted in Scripture. When you don't know God's Word intimately, you have no standard to test spiritual experiences against. You're relying on feelings and impressions—which are easily manipulated by the enemy.

Third: Because they're not in an intimate, daily relationship with God. They know about God but don't truly **KNOW** Him. They haven't learned to recognize His voice, His presence, His **PEACE**. So when a counterfeit shows up, they can't tell the difference.

Fourth: Because they opened doors. Knowingly or unknowingly, they participated in practices that gave the enemy legal access. Maybe it was "just for fun" at a party. Maybe it was "innocent curiosity." Maybe it was a desperate moment when they turned to the wrong source for answers. But doors were opened, and now the enemy has access he shouldn't have.

Fifth: Because God allows free will. He doesn't force protection on people who choose to venture into enemy territory. If you willingly walk into a minefield, God isn't obligated to miraculously remove all the mines. He warns. He convicts. He calls you back. But He doesn't override your choices.

"But I prayed about it first! I asked God to protect me!"

Let me ask you something. If you prayed for protection and then walked into oncoming traffic on purpose, would you expect to survive?

Prayer doesn't sanctify disobedience. You can't pray a blessing over sin and expect God to honor it. You can't ask for protection while deliberately walking into enemy territory.

That's not how it works here.

That's not how any of this works anywhere or anytime.

REMEMBER YOUR ADVERSARY

Your adversary, the devil / Satan / Lucifer / the god of this world, is looking to distract, fool, confuse, torment, oppress, possess, and eventually destroy you.

"Be alert and of sober mind [vigilant and cautious] at all times. Because your **enemy [adversary]**, **the devil, prowls [roams] around** like a roaring lion **looking for someone to seize upon** and **devour**." (1 Peter 5:8)

To this point, we've discussed the many, many ways he's trying to do these things to everyone in the world. And unfortunately, he's been very successful.

He's been doing this for thousands of years. He's watched every generation. He's studied human psychology long before humans invented the term. He knows our weaknesses, our desires, our vulnerabilities.

He knows that humans crave spiritual connection.

He knows that humans want to feel special, chosen, gifted.

He knows that humans are easily impressed by supernatural experiences.

And he uses ALL of it against us.

You mean, "the devil doesn't have my best interest at heart?"

No duh! No double duh!

THE ONLY WAY TO BE SURE

As taught in my first book, *THE DAILY STAND*, you can **ONLY** be sure by:

First: By having **met the Lord personally**; and having a living, personal, daily, intimate relationship with Him. Not knowing about God—**actually knowing Him. Talking** to Him. **Listening** to Him. **Walking** with Him moment by moment.

Second: By consistently studying God's Word / Bible / Scriptures along with the original texts. Not just listening to teachers, preachers, ministers or leaders and taking their word for it. "Study to show yourself approved." Know what God actually says, not what people say He says.

Third: By **abiding in Christ** [**in The Anointing**]. Living in that place of continual surrender and connection. Not visiting God on Sundays—dwelling with Him always.

Fourth: By having the **Anointing** of the **Holy Spirit flowing through you** from your innermost being and confirming everything. That inner witness that says "Yes" or "No" before your mind even processes what's happening.

Fifth: By having **THE PEACE** of God that passes understanding and comprehension guarding your heart and mind in Christ. This **PEACE** is not an emotion—it's a supernatural indicator. When something is from God, **THE PEACE** is present. When something is not from God, **THE PEACE** lifts. Learn to recognize this.

Sixth: By having the **unmistakable Love** and **Joy that comes directly from God**, the Father, flowing in and through you. Along with seeing the fruits of the [Holy] Spirit flowing in, through, and around your life.

When you can see, feel, and have these things in and around you in a real dynamic way—then you can be sure.

TESTING THE SPIRITS

"Beloved, **do not believe every spirit**, but **test the spirits** to see **whether they are from God**, because many false prophets have gone out into the world." (1 John 4:1)

We're commanded to test the spirits. Not accept every spiritual experience as legitimate. Not assume that supernatural equals divine. Not trust our feelings as the final arbiter of truth.

How do we test?

By asking:

Does this align with Scripture? **ALL** of Scripture, not just the parts I want to hear?

Does this glorify Jesus Christ as Lord and Savior? Or does it minimize Him, redefine Him, or put something else at the center?

Does this produce the fruit of the Spirit—love, joy, peace, patience, kindness, goodness, faithfulness, gentleness, self-control? Or does it produce pride, confusion, fear, judgement, anger, wrath, or bondage?

Does **THE PEACE** confirm it? That deep, unmistakable, supernatural peace that guards your heart and mind?

Does it draw me closer to God or further from Him? Does it increase my dependence on Christ or on something else?

WHY SO MANY

COUNTERFEITS?

And Why do They Look SO GOOD?

Why?

Let me go on a little tangent for a minute that will help answer this question.

We need to understand the simple truth: The reason counterfeits exist is **ONLY** because the real thing existed first. People wouldn't print counterfeit $100 bills unless the real $100 bill already existed, and they were worth a LOT.

The enemy is creating counterfeits because the **REAL** things from God do exist. He's only counterfeiting those things that would excite us in the spiritual realm that a true believer can have with God; in the same way a large stash of $100 bills would be exciting in the natural realm.

That's why it's so tricky to talk about this area. Remember Jesus talked about all the false prophets, as well as what we covered in 1 John 4:1. It's because the real prophetic exists. In Chapter Four, we discussed what "prophet" and "prophetic" really mean. And how both God and the enemy will use it.

Therefore, the enemy will create counterfeits. And why not, because the prophetic, for example, can seem so exciting and becomes an easy way for him to invade the lives of Christians who want to touch the spiritual realm.

I told you in Chapter Four, "'Prophetic' art workshops are teaching Christians to paint and draw while in altered states, believing they're channeling images from God. Students are instructed to empty their minds, surrender control, and let 'the Spirit' guide their hands. What they're actually doing is practicing automatic art—a classic occult technique where demons control human actions."

So, let's look at the differences:

"Altered states" are a definite NO.

"Channeling" is a definite NO.

So, while "surrendering control to Jesus" and "letting the Holy Spirit guide" are normal and REAL things Christian believers should do; in this setting they're FALSE and COUNERFEIT. Because when these things are premised with "altered states" and "channeling," it makes the next statements become FALSE—again by opening up to the wrong spirits.

These would be the same counterfeits versus REAL in the areas of "soaking prayer" and "contemplative prayer" that empties your mind—creating a passive state—waiting for "spirits" to fill it, instead of filling it by Scripture.

So in all these cases, it's the **emptying of the mind** and **waiting on "spirits" to fill a vacuum** that's FALSE and COUNERFEIT; versus "be still and know that I'm God" (Psalm 46:10), "those who wait on the Lord" (Isaiah 40:31), and "taking every thought captive into the obedience of [yielding to] Christ [the Anointing]" (2 Corinthians 10:5). All the latter are **ACTIVE places** in the REAL Truth of God's Word. When we wait on the Lord and rest in Him, taking all our thoughts [by yielding] to Him, is **NOT** going into an "altered state" with a "totally empty mind." This is far different from giving our thoughts over to the Lord and waiting in His Presence just to be with Him; and then hear from Him.

Okay, I'm back.

So Why are There so Many Counterfeits?

Because every single counterfeit the enemy has is telling you that God actually has a Real gift and a Real spiritual experience—not these fake ones—planned for **EVERYONE** who will give up their **ALL** to follow Him alone.

The enemy doesn't want you to find an intimate relationship with the One, True God and then experience His REAL Truth and Life with Him. And he'll do anything to confuse or divert you.

But for you to find them, you must remember the "how to be sure" and all the "tests" you've been learning here.

The Pendulum Swing

As a last-ditch effort: The enemy hopes that if you reject him, his fake spirituality, and his counterfeits because of what you learn in this book; that at least, you'll also reject God and His REAL Truth in the spiritual world that He has for you.

THE BOTTOM LINE

The spiritual realm is real

Your desire to connect to it is legitimate—God put it there.

But there is **ONLY** one safe, legitimate, God-honoring way to access it: through Jesus Christ, by the power of the Holy Spirit, in alignment with the Word of God, confirmed by **THE PEACE**.

Every other doorway leads to the same place—enemy territory.

It might feel good at first.

It might seem helpful.

It might produce "results."

But the destination is always the same: deeper bondage, spiritual oppression, and separation from the God who actually loves you.

The way is narrow.

The gate is narrow.

Few find it.

Don't be one of the many who take the broad road because it's easier, because it offers more options, because it doesn't require surrender.

Be one of the few.

Walk the narrow way.

Find the narrow gate.

It's the ONLY way that leads to life.

CHAPTER TEN

NEW AGE AND NEW THOUGHT IN THE CHURCH

SOME NEW AGE TEACHINGS HAVE BEEN WIDELY ACCEPTED IN MANY CHURCHES

This is Where the Masquerade's Deception Actually Gets Personal

In God's beloved Church.

In your church.

Maybe even in You.

T HESE BELIEFS HAVE BECOME widely accepted in the Christian world.

With many of God's people and church environments, these principles don't need to be marketed—they're accepted outright as fact.

In many, many others, they've been put under religious masks with religious words and sometimes the distorted use of the Scriptures to make these principles palatable, believable, and "sold" as "God's Truth."

Because nothing says "biblical Christianity" quite like ancient Hindu meditation techniques rebranded as "contemplative prayer."

Or Eastern mysticism dressed up in Christian vocabulary.

Or New Age manifestation principles sold as "speaking faith."

Slap a Bible verse on it and suddenly it's "Christian."

Right?

Wrong.

All of these are under the guise of those who are truly spiritually discerning—and only those who have their spiritual eyes opened can see them. Defining others who require strict interpretation of the Scriptures with **NO** room to "expand" or "grow" as spiritually lacking and close-minded.

"The Law of Attraction"

As mentioned previously:

We are one with god.

We are mini-gods.

We are god.

Along with whatever we give out into the world, we'll get it back.

Karma.

This law champions the principle that "like attracts like". Advocating positive thoughts attracts positive outcomes. Promoting the belief that it makes the individual their own god by claiming power to control universal forces through mental techniques.

"For My thoughts are not your thoughts, neither are your ways My ways, says the Lord. For as the heavens are higher than the earth, so are My ways higher than your ways and My thoughts than your thoughts." (Isaiah 55:8-9)

"But Tom, I'm just being positive! What's wrong with positive thinking?"

Nothing—if you're actually just thinking positively.

Everything—if you think your positive thoughts have the power to manipulate the universe and force outcomes.

That's not positive thinking.

That's playing god. And last time I checked, that position is already filled.

"Oneness"

Since we are one with god and we are god, then we must all be one—whether we understand that or not.

Therefore, we must do whatever it takes to become one. Including teaching the "uninformed" this "truth" so they can join our oneness in god.

This stands in contrast and as a counterfeit to the Scriptures in many ways.

First: As discussed in previous chapters, we clearly defined that we cannot become a god or mini-god. That's just deception from the god of this world.

Second: The definition of true unity from the Scriptures is singular and only comes by being in God Himself. Such as in:

"I do not ask on behalf of these alone, but for those also who believe in Me through their word; that **they may all be one**; even as You, Father, are in Me and I in You, that **they also may be in Us**, so that the world may believe that You sent Me." (John 17:20-21)

True biblical unity is found IN God—not by becoming god.

"Religious Pluralism"

Which teaches no one is wrong. And **ALL** paths lead to god. And for those who don't accept this, such as Bible-centric Christians who narrowly state that "Jesus is the Only way", they are intolerant.

They utilize this teaching to redefine what being a Christian means to them.

Of course us stupid Christians who actually believe the Bible is the word of God, are just dumb enough to believe Jesus when he said, "I AM The [ONLY] Way and The [ONLY] Truth and The [ONLY] Life; NO ONE comes to the Father except by [through] Me."

"Tom, you're so intolerant! How dare you say there's only one way!"

I didn't say it. Jesus did.

Take it up with Him.

"Universalism"

Which states all are or will be saved, no matter what. All are children of god. And Jesus is not the ONLY way. He's just one of many ways to reach god.

Yet we've covered this previously as the exclusivity of salvation is clearly stated in Acts 4:12: "Salvation is found in NO ONE else, for there is NO OTHER name under heaven given to mankind by which we must be saved."

"Mysticism"

Which Teaches if you seek god through all means, within all spiritual avenues, you'll get extra secrets that others will never get. Mysticism is a lust for the supernatural; for power; and for spirituality. Emphasizing that those who don't utilize all the opportunities made available to them will never understand nor get such.

This sounds appealing, doesn't it? Secret knowledge. Hidden wisdom. Spiritual experiences that the "ordinary" believers will never have.

That's exactly why it's so dangerous.

New Age is Progressive Christianity.

UNDERSTAND THIS

There is no desire among New Age and New Thought devotees to know the limits of the straight and narrow path that advocates having a limited small gate of entrance.

Again, from Matthew 7:13-14, "Enter through the **narrow gate**; for the gate is wide and the way is broad that leads to destruction, and there are many who enter through it. For the **gate is small** and the **way is narrow** that leads to life, and there are few who find it."

Those who buy into and believe New Age and New Thought [and the masquerade of spiritual forces behind them] would claim I and those who believe this way are narrow-minded.

But if God is God, then they are wrong.

They call us narrow-minded, like it's an insult.

Jesus called the way "narrow" as if it's a fact.

I'll take His word for it.

They want to believe their "version of god" that they created in their minds is the truth. Notice the words "they created." It's exactly like the man-made false Belief Systems we discussed in *SET THE CAPTIVES FREE*. Where men, backed by demon rulers, created these Belief Systems and then defined them as the Truth. At which point, they then expect others to live by their newly created, narrow set of beliefs.

They choose to live in "ignorant bliss." They don't study their Bibles and the original Greek and Hebrew texts to learn for themselves, as the Bereans did.

"Now these [the Bereans] were more noble-minded than those in

Thessalonica, for they received the word with great eagerness, **examining the Scriptures daily to see whether these things were so."** (Acts 17:11)

NEW AGE PRACTICES THAT HAVE INFILTRATED CHURCHES

Let me be specific about what's actually happening in churches across the world—practices that have been "Christianized" but remain rooted in New Age and Eastern mysticism.

Contemplative Prayer / Centering Prayer

This practice teaches believers to empty their minds, repeat a sacred word or phrase (mantra), and enter an altered state of consciousness to "experience God." It's promoted by authors like Richard Foster, Thomas Merton, and Henri Nouwen.

The problem? It's Transcendental Meditation with a Christian label. Emptying your mind doesn't invite God in—it opens you to whatever spirit wants to fill the void.

Biblical prayer is engaging with God—talking to Him, listening to Him, thinking His thoughts after Him. Not emptying your mind and waiting for "something" to happen.

Yoga in Churches

"Christian Yoga" or "Holy Yoga" has become increasingly popular. Churches offer yoga classes as "outreach" or "fitness ministry."

Here's what they don't tell you: Yoga was designed for union with Hindu deities. The poses are worship positions to Hindu gods. The breathing techniques are designed to awaken "kundalini"—the serpent power. You cannot separate yoga from its spiritual roots any more than you can separate Communion from Christ.

Calling it "Christian" doesn't change what it is. It just makes the deception more palatable.

"But I'm just stretching! It's just exercise!"

Then stretch. Do Pilates. Go for a walk.

Why are you doing worship positions to Hindu gods and calling it Christianity?

The Enneagram

This personality typing system has swept through churches, seminaries, and Christian organizations. It's used for "spiritual formation," leadership development, and personal growth.

The origins? Armenian-Greek mystic and occultist George Gurdjieff. Bolivian mystic Oscar Ichazo. Chilean psychiatrist Claudio Naranjo. Automatic writing from demonic entities. Channeled revelation. Then brought into Christian circles by Catholic mystics, who mixed it with contemplative spirituality.

Your identity is not found in a number on a personality chart. Your identity is found **IN CHRIST**.

Breath Prayers

Taught as a way to "pray without ceasing," breath prayers involve repeating a short phrase coordinated with breathing—inhale on one word, exhale on another.

This is mantra meditation. It induces an altered state of consciousness. The repetition of words to achieve a spiritual state is exactly what Jesus warned against: "And when you are praying, **do not use meaningless repetition** as the Gentiles do, for they suppose that they will be heard for their many words." (Matthew 6:7)

Soaking Prayer

Lying still, often with instrumental music, "soaking in God's presence" for extended periods. Practitioners are told to empty their minds and "receive."

Again—emptying your mind is not biblical. It's Eastern mysticism. And it opens doors to the wrong spirits. The "presence" you're soaking in may not be God at all.

CO-CREATING WITH THE UNIVERSE

Co-Creating is a belief that humans are divine partners with cosmic forces in creating reality. It denies God's sovereignty while promoting self-deification through spiritual techniques.

MINDSET

Is the belief that changing thought patterns can directly alter external circumstances through spiritual laws. It's a subtle form of manifestation disguised as psychology.

Mindset promotes personal power over submission to God.

As well as identity shifting by just using your mind to change in how you perceive yourself and thereby create the existence you want. Believing that by adopting a different set of beliefs, values, or behaviors which align with a new identity you want to embody will make it become true.

"I'm just renewing my mind like the Bible says!"

No, you're not.

Romans 12:2 says to be transformed by the renewing of your mind—**according to God's Word** and **by His Spirit**. **NOT** by your own mental techniques to create your own reality.

There's a big difference between aligning your mind with God's Truth and trying to use your mind to manipulate the universe.

ABUNDANCE MINDSET

This is the philosophy that focusing on wealth and success will attract material prosperity. Often mixed with the biblical "prosperity gospel" to create "Christian manifestation" practices. ALL GARBAGE when you realize what True Faith is—walking with the One and Only, True God as clearly laid out in *THE DAILY STAND*.

Christian Manifestation

The entire premise is a deception which combines spiritual concepts with manifestation practices. Claiming to have tapped into the truth, which allows the enlightened to align personal desires with "soul purpose" to manifest outcomes through spiritual force.

"Manifestation and reality creation" is an advanced belief that enlightened humans can literally create their own physical reality through consciousness and spiritual techniques. This becomes the ultimate expression of human pride and self-deification.

ALL THESE PRACTICES SHARE COMMON CHARACTERISTICS

Self-deification: Making humans into gods.

Rejection of biblical authority: Creating personal spiritual systems.

Spirit contact: Opening doors to demonic influence.

Pride: Claiming they now have the power that belongs only to God.

And, **Deception**: Promising godlike abilities to fallen humans.

But We Were Warned:

"But I am afraid that as the serpent deceived Eve by his cunning, **your thoughts will be led astray** from a sincere and pure devotion to Christ." (2 Corinthians 11:3)

Remember:

If God, the Father, won't answer these prayers, the god of this world gladly will.

Only Through a True Relationship:

With God the Father, Jesus Christ, and the Holy Spirit, are humans able to access True authentic spiritual power, healing, and transformation. None of this is available through manipulation of cosmic forces or self-deification techniques.

DIVINE GOD AND GODDESS

When people use those titles for themselves, it shows the deep level of deception they've fallen into.

This goes beyond chasing after all the false doctrines of demon spirits and believing that they can someday attain becoming a mini-god. Instead, they now actually believe they are a divine god or divine goddess. When people fall for this new level of deception, it will become something even harder to return from.

"I am a divine goddess!"

No, you're not. You're a created being who has bought the same lie Satan has been selling since Eden: "You will be like God."

How did that work out for the people who believed it then?

THE ENLIGHTENED MIND ~ LIVING ON A HIGHER PLANE

"The Next Great Revelations"

This is where the lines cross. Where the water becomes very muddy. Where people are deceived into believing they have the next "Great Revelations" from God. They have a secret that no one else knows. These are Great Deceptions put on believers in the Church.

"But the [Holy] Spirit distinctly and expressly declares that in latter times

some will turn away from the faith, giving attention to **deluding** and **seducing spirits** and **doctrines that demons teach**." (1 Timothy 4:1)

SPEAKING THINGS INTO EXISTENCE

The Counterfeits vs The Real

Let's start with The Counterfeits

We've defined much about the counterfeits to this point. Therefore, I won't reiterate it all—but it goes back to "visualization" and "manifestation."

In these teachings, when people are connecting to the wrong spirits, they use the technique of visualizing what they want and the technique of manifesting to achieve it. Convinced by just speaking whatever they want to say and believe is enough—when "connected into the universe"—they'll create it out of the same. As if they are now "mini-gods."

Unfortunately, the True and Living God will not answer those manmade, demon-backed techniques. He won't honor such garbage. Yet the god of this world is more than happy to do so. The devil loves putting on "dog and pony shows" and is more than glad to answer all so he can keep leading (even good believers) down the wrong path. Hoping to gain ground—to ruin their lives.

Many times, good believers have been deceived into believing that they can "speaking into existence" what they think is the right thing. They might even use and speak the scriptures to convince themselves they're doing the right thing. But in these cases, the written word is **NOT** enough. It **MUST** be the Living Word, as we'll see in a moment.

The Real

The Real differs from the counterfeits because it **ONLY** happens when we speak forth the Living Word from the True and Living God that He's saying in the moment. It's exactly the same as when Jesus walked and said, **"I ONLY do what I see my Father doing and I ONLY say what I hear my Father saying."** (John 5:19; John 5:30; John 14:31)

Jesus said [**ONLY**] **IF** [and **WHEN**] we had Real, True faith, [**THEN**, and only then] "Truly I tell you, if anyone says to this mountain, Go, throw yourself into the sea, and does not doubt in their heart but believes that what they say will happen, it will be done for them." (Mark 11:22–23)

This is one of many verses the "name it and claim it" Faith Movement ("faithers") project as part of their foundational deceit. They love to promote faith as something that they can use to manipulate God and receive divine responses by just projecting manmade levels of "THEIR faith." They focus on the many verses that include the statement, "if you only had faith, you could..." do "such and such." Championing that if we just try hard enough... if we just muster up enough of OUR faith... we can move God.

Which is spiritual CRAP.

"Tom you're wrong. I've been taught that if I just have enough faith, the Bible says I can speak anything into existence!"

No. You can't.

You haven't learned the whole picture yet.

Faith is not a force you manipulate. Faith is trusting God—His character, His Word, His timing—and knowing Him and His will for each moment. Not demanding your desires by projecting "enough faith" to force His hand.

There's a massive difference between faith that trusts God and "faith" that tries to control God.

The Faith Movement is not only a powerful movement that infiltrated New Age and New Thought, but many other churches and teachings as well.

Why?

Because once again, it appeals to our flesh. To being able to obtain spiritual control. To our pride. To being "mini-gods" that can speak things into existence. This is the epitome of power.

Yet these scriptures are not "willy-nilly" statements that deceived believers in the Church can throw around and make ["wish"] believe that it'll happen—if we only could muster up enough of OUR faith. This is one of the many times when Jesus spoke in parables or with hidden meanings that the simple observers would never understand. It takes an intimate walk with the True and Living God to understand what is **hidden in plain sight**.

Instead, this describes **Real Faith**, as I define it in great detail in the chapter *"Real Faith, True Faith"* in **THE DAILY STAND**. Please go back and study that information presented there before thinking God gave us "cart blanche" freedom to go do anything we want "in OUR faith"; as the "name it and claim it" Faith Movement (faither) folks promote we can do.

This is the same deception at the heart of the "prosperity gospel."

While there may be some New Age/New Thought people who would distance themselves from the Faith Movement to convince others that they're different; their visualizing, speaking, and manifesting "whatevers" is the **EXACT** same thing as the faithers' "name it and claim it" BS.

THE BOTTOM LINE

The New Age has infiltrated the Church.

It came wearing Christian clothes, speaking Christian words, quoting Christian Scripture.

But underneath the disguise, it's the same old lies from the same old enemy: You can be like God. You have the power. You don't need to submit—you can create your own reality.

Whether it's called "manifestation" or "faith confession"...

Whether it's called "centering prayer" or "meditation"...

Whether it's called "divine feminine" or "goddess spirituality"...

It's the same deception in different packaging.

Only through a genuine intimate relationship with God the Father, Jesus Christ, and the Holy Spirit, are humans able to access true authentic spiritual power, healing, and transformation. None of this is available through manipulation of cosmic forces or self-deification techniques.

Test everything against Scripture.

Confirm everything with THE PEACE.

Stay on the narrow path.

Because the broad road is very crowded—and it doesn't lead where you want to go.

CHAPTER ELEVEN

ALL MYSTICISM IS BS

THIS IS TRUE 100% OF THE TIME—NO EXCEPTIONS

A MERICA AND THE WORLD have fully embraced mystical practices and spiritualism.

It's everywhere. In your bookstore. In your yoga studio. In your therapy sessions. In your corporate team-building retreats. In your kids' schools. On your social media feeds.

And yes—in your churches.

Because nothing screams "spiritual enlightenment" quite like ancient demonic practices repackaged with trendy vocabulary and a good marketing budget.

"Mindfulness." "Transcendence." "Higher consciousness." "Awakening."

Same garbage. New wrapper.

WHAT IS MYSTICISM?

Mysticism is:

1. Belief in direct experience of transcendent reality or God, especially by means of contemplation and asceticism instead of rational thought.

2. Such experience had by an individual.

3. Belief in the existence of realities beyond perceptual or intellectual apprehension that are directly accessible by subjective experience. A belief in séances, astral projection, and similar mysticism.

4. Belief that is not based on evidence or subjected to criticism.

5. Obscurity of doctrine.

6. The doctrine of the Mystics, who professed a pure, sublime, and wholly disinterested devotion, and maintained that they had direct intercourse with the divine Spirit, and acquired a knowledge of God and of spiritual things unattainable by the natural intellect, and such as cannot be analyzed or explained.

7. The doctrine that the ultimate elements or principles of knowledge or belief are gained by an act or process akin to feeling or faith.

8. The beliefs, ideas, or thoughts of mystics.

As quoted from "The American Heritage® Dictionary of the English Language, 5th Edition"

The Heart of Mysticism

The basic definition and belief in Mysticism is the pursuit of direct, personal experience of ultimate reality, the divine, or absolute truth through contemplation, spiritual practices, or altered states of consciousness, typically transcending ordinary perception and rational understanding.

Mysticism appears in many religions and philosophies. Mystics seek union with or immediate knowledge of the sacred—whether that's God (in theistic traditions), enlightenment (in Hinduism, Buddhism, Taoism, and Sufism), or cosmic consciousness (in various spiritual systems). Common elements include meditation, prayer, ascetic practices, and experiences described as unspeakable, transformative encounters that reveal hidden dimensions of existence.

The mystical path emphasizes experiential knowing over doctrinal belief or intellectual study alone. Once again, seeking experience with **NO** boundaries, such as the Word of God.

"But Tom, I'm just seeking a deeper spiritual experience! What's wrong with wanting to know God more intimately?"

Nothing—if you're seeking God through the way He prescribed.

Everything—if you're seeking spiritual experiences through any means available, bypassing Scripture, bypassing Christ, bypassing the Holy Spirit, and opening yourself to whatever "transcendent reality" shows up.

Guess what's going to show up?

Not God.

MYSTICISM COMES IN

MANY FLAVORS

Most Eastern Religions practice some kind of mysticism. But there's also Jewish mysticism. Islamic mysticism. Christian mysticism. And, as we learned earlier, Quantum mysticism.

Hindu Mysticism — Seeks union with Brahman through yoga, meditation, and kundalini awakening. The goal is to realize that your individual soul (your "Atman") is identical with the universal soul.

Buddhist Mysticism — Seeks enlightenment through meditation, mindfulness, and the dissolution of the ego. The goal is to escape the cycle of rebirth and achieve nirvana.

Sufi Mysticism — The mystical branch of Islam seeking a direct experience of Allah through whirling, chanting, and ecstatic practices.

Kabbalah (Jewish Mysticism) — Seeks hidden knowledge of God through esoteric interpretation of Scripture, numerology, and meditation on divine names.

Christian Mysticism — Claims to seek direct union with God through contemplative prayer, but often borrows heavily from Eastern practices. Desert fathers, medieval mystics, and modern contemplatives all fall into this category.

Quantum Mysticism — The modern attempt to hijack physics to "prove" that consciousness creates reality and we are all connected to a universal mind. Dressed in scientific vocabulary to sound credible.

"But Christian mysticism is different! It's about knowing God!"

Is it though?

When you empty your mind instead of filling it with Scripture...

When you seek experience instead of obedience...

When you pursue altered states of consciousness instead of the renewal of your mind...

You're not practicing Christianity. You're practicing Eastern mysticism with a Christian vocabulary.

THE PROBLEM WITH ALL MYSTICISM

On the surface, seeking God through any means should lead to good.

Right?

Wrong.

Mysticism is NEVER from God

Aren't there exceptions?

NO.

Why?

Simply because the very heart of mysticism is manmade beliefs and pursuits of the divine by human efforts—which we now know and can see are backed by demon rulers.

Let me break this down:

First: Mysticism seeks experience without boundaries. It doesn't submit to Scripture. It doesn't test spirits. It doesn't require that experiences align with the written Word of God. It just pursues "the divine" through whatever means seem to work.

Second: Mysticism bypasses Christ. Jesus said, "I am **THE Way**." Not "a" way. Not "one of many" ways. **THE Way**. Mysticism says, "There are many paths to the divine." That's a direct contradiction of Jesus' own words.

Third: Mysticism opens doors to the demonic. When you empty your mind, you create a vacancy. When you seek "ANY spiritual experience," you invite "ANY spirit" to provide it. And the spirits that answer are NOT the Holy Spirit.

Fourth: Mysticism elevates human effort over divine grace. It's about what you do to reach God—your meditation, your contemplation, your practices—rather than what God has done to reach you through Christ.

Fifth: Mysticism produces counterfeit experiences. The "transcendent encounters" feel real. The "divine presence" seems authentic. **But feelings are not truth**. And the enemy is very good at providing convincing counterfeits.

"But I had such a powerful experience! It felt so real! It changed my life!"

I don't doubt that.

The question isn't whether the experience was real. The question is:

What was the source?

Because the enemy can produce powerful experiences too. He's been doing it for thousands of years. He's very, very good at it.

THERE IS ONLY ONE WAY

Once again, it goes back to John 14:6:

Jesus is the ONLY way.

NOT Jesus PLUS meditation.

NOT Jesus PLUS contemplative prayer.

NOT Jesus PLUS mystical experiences.

NOT Jesus PLUS altered states of consciousness.

Just Jesus.

Through His Word. By His Spirit. In relationship with Him. Walking with Him daily, moment by moment, listening to His voice, following His leading, confirmed by **THE PEACE**.

That's it. That's the path. That's the narrow gate.

AND EVERYTHING ELSE?

Is just PURE GARBAGE!

I don't say this to be harsh.

I say this because I've seen the destruction.

I've seen sincere believers get sucked into mystical practices, thinking they were getting closer to God, only to find themselves further from Him than ever.

I've seen people open doors to the demonic through "innocent" spiritual practices and spend years trying to get free.

I've seen churches embrace mysticism and watch their people drift into deception, confusion, and spiritual bondage.

The enemy doesn't care what label you put on it. Christian mysticism. Contemplative prayer. Spiritual formation. Sacred practices.

He just cares that you're opening doors you shouldn't open.

Seeking experiences instead of Truth.

Bypassing Christ to find "the divine."

There is ONLY One God

One way to reach Him.

One name by which we must be saved.

Jesus.

Everything else—no matter how spiritual it feels, no matter how "Christian" it sounds, no matter how profound the experience—is...

Evil's Great Masquerade.

Period.

CHAPTER TWELVE

TYPES OF CAPTIVITY

DIFFICULT TO IGNORE

I hope this book is difficult for you.

Not difficult to read.

Difficult to ignore.

WHY? BECAUSE WE'VE COVERED a lot of ground. We're pulling back the curtain on the Evil's Great Masquerade. We're exposing the enemy's tactics, his counterfeits, his lies dressed up in spiritual clothing.

And now it's time to name what's at stake.

Captivity.

"But Tom, I'm a Christian! I can't be held captive!"

Really?

Then why are so many believers stuck? Bound? Going in circles? Feeling distant from God? Confused about what's true? Chasing experiences instead of the One who gives life?

Captivity doesn't always look like physical chains. Sometimes it looks like a comfortable life that's completely disconnected from God's purpose. Sometimes it looks like "spiritual growth" that's actually leading further from Truth.

Sometimes it looks like church.

THE TYPES WE'VE EXPOSED

We've defined a lot in this book. Let's review:

All types of captivity, all avenues of bondage, all roads that lead away from the One True God—they fall into the categories we've covered:

False Anointings

Counterfeit spiritual power that mimics the real thing. People experience "something"—manifestations, feelings, experiences—but it's not from the Holy Spirit. It's from the other side, dressed up to look legitimate.

The tragedy? Many never question the source. If it feels spiritual, it must be God.

Right?

Wrong. Dead wrong.

False Spiritual Experiences

Encounters that feel profound, transformative, even life-changing—but they're not from God. They're from the enemy, who is more than happy to provide powerful experiences to those seeking them through the wrong doors.

Mystical experiences. Altered states of consciousness. "Encounters" with beings of "light." Visions. Dreams that seem prophetic. All available from the counterfeit spiritual realm.

False Angels

Demons masquerading as angels of light—just as Scripture warned us. They appear helpful. They offer guidance. They seem holy.

But their guidance leads away from Christ, not toward Him. Their "revelations" contradict Scripture. Their fruit is confusion, bondage, and distance from the True God.

"And no wonder, for Satan himself **masquerades as an angel of light**. It is not surprising, then, if his servants **also masquerade as servants of righteousness**." (2 Corinthians 11:14-15)

False Spiritual Beliefs

The doctrines of demons taught as truth. New Age philosophy dressed in Christian vocabulary. Man-made belief systems backed by spiritual forces of darkness.

We've covered them: The Law of Attraction. Oneness. Religious Pluralism. Universalism. Mysticism. Manifestation. Co-creating with the universe. All of it—garbage disguised as enlightenment.

Self-Healing

The belief that you have the power within yourself to heal your body, mind, and spirit. Energy healing. Chakra balancing. Crystal therapy. Reiki. All claiming you can tap into "universal energy" to heal yourself.

The Truth?

Real healing comes from God. And what's being channeled in these practices isn't neutral energy—it's demonic power that brings bondage, not freedom.

Self-Manifestations

Speaking things into existence through your own power. Visualizing your desires into reality. "Creating" your life through thought and intention.

Whether it's called manifestation or "faith confession," it's the same lie: You have godlike power to create reality. You don't need to submit to God's will—you can impose your own.

Self-Belief

The ultimate deception: Believing in yourself as the source of truth, power, and transformation. "You are enough." "Trust yourself." "You have everything you need within you."

It sounds empowering. It's actually the original lie from the Garden: "You will be like God." And it leads to the same destination—separation from the One who actually is enough.

ALL BACKED BY DEMONS

Every single one.

No exceptions.

I know that sounds harsh. I know some people reading this are thinking, "But my experience felt so good! My practice has helped me so much! My beliefs have brought me peace!"

And I'm telling you—that's exactly how the enemy operates.

He doesn't show up with horns and a pitchfork. He shows up with peace, power, experiences, and "a truth" that feels so right.

Until you realize you're further from God than when you started.

Until you realize the "freedom" you found is actually a different kind of bondage.

Until you realize the "light" you've been following is darkness disguised.

"But surely NOT all of it is demonic! Some of it must be neutral, right?"

No.

There is no neutral ground in the spiritual realm. You're either connected to the True God through Jesus Christ by the Holy Spirit, or you're connected to the counterfeit.

In Luke 11:23, Jesus said, "**WHOEVER** is **NOT** with Me is **AGAINST** Me."

There's no middle option. There's no spiritual Switzerland. There's NO such thing as being a "happy agnostic." There's no "harmless" alternative spirituality.

If it's not from God, it's from the other side.

Period.

THE MANY WHO NEED FREEDOM

With the original two books, and now, with what we've covered here in this book, we can see many others. It all comes down to the many, many people needing freedom from the many, many false spiritual avenues they're on. And the bondages and captivity they've come under—by choice—knowingly or not.

Think about it:

How many people are trapped in New Age beliefs, thinking they're on a path to enlightenment?

How many Christians have embraced practices that opened doors to the demonic without even knowing it?

How many seekers are chasing spiritual experiences that lead further from the Truth?

How many sincere people are following false angels they believe are from God?

How many are manifesting, visualizing, and "believing" their way into deeper bondage?

Millions.

Maybe Billions.

And they all need to be set free.

NAME THE MANY

The many covered in this book to this point:

Those trapped in Quantum Mysticism and the lie that consciousness creates reality.

Those deceived by counterfeit miracles, signs, and wonders.

Those who've opened portals through occult practices—knowingly or unknowingly.

Those bound by energy healing, Reiki, chakra work, and "universal life force."

Those seeking direct lines to the spirit realm through doors God never authorized.

Those caught up in the New Age and New Thought that has infiltrated the Church.

Those pursuing ALL forms of mysticism—which we've established is 100% BS, with NO exceptions.

Those captive to the Evil's Great Masquerade in ALL its forms.

ALL of them need freedom.

ALL of them can find freedom.

But only through the One who said, "I am THE Way, THE Truth, and THE Life."

Not through more techniques.

Not through better practices.

Not through deeper experiences.

Through Jesus. Only Jesus. Always Jesus.

Everything else is just another form of captivity wearing a different mask.

CHAPTER THIRTEEN

THE ROAD IS NARROW

THAT LEADS TO LIFE ~ BROAD IS THE WAY THAT LEADS TO DESTRUCTION

I'M NOT GOING TO quote John 14:6 again. I'll simply say very clearly: **Jesus is the ONLY way.**

No ifs, ands, or buts—no matter how "narrow" that statement might seem.

Now it's time to concentrate on Matthew 7:13-14.

"**Enter through the Narrow Gate**; for the **gate is wide** and the **way is broad** that **leads to destruction**, and there are **MANY** who enter through it. For the **Gate is Small** and the **Way is Narrow** that **Leads to Life**, and there are **FEW** who find it."

Look. **ALL** false spiritualities described in this book are on an extremely broad road with a wide gate at its end. **ALL** of Woo's paths lead to the same destruction. Eternity away from the One and Only, True and Living God.

"But Tom, that sounds so harsh! So exclusive! So judgmental!"

I'm not here to preach "hell fire and brimstone." I'm here to inform you that as long as you're alive here on the Earth, you have a choice.

Choose wisely.

Whether that's burning in hell or living in outer darkness—who cares? It won't be fun—**EVER**—from that time forward. And in every sense of the word, it'll be horrible.

CHASING A MILLION DIFFERENT ANSWERS A MILLION DIFFERENT WAYS

While many are chasing a million different answers in a million different ways, there's only **ONE**.

ALL the Greatest Mysteries, Wisdom, Understandings, Secrets of God, the Universe, and **EVERYTHING** in the spiritual realm are revealed inside **ONE Simple Truth**: being **IN CHRIST**. Hence, we need to learn how to live our lives in the Presence and by the Heart of the Father, Papa God.

"That's it? That's too simple!"

Exactly.

The enemy wants you to believe the truth is complicated, hidden, requiring special knowledge, advanced techniques, years of study, secret initiations.

God says: Come to Me through My Son. That's it.

Simple enough for a child. Offensive to those who think they need to earn their way to enlightenment.

TANGENTS IN THE CHURCH

Sidelined on a Side Road

A great way for the enemy to sideline believers is to get them on tangents. Physical tangents. Mental tangents. Emotional tangents. Physiological tangents. Spiritual tangents.

Anything to keep believers from walking the narrow road with Papa God.

Do you remember "The Church of No Tangents" from **SET THE CAPTIVES FREE**? Where I told the joke we used to make about that "church."

The bottom line of that story was we were so determined to make sure we didn't go on any tangents EVER again that we ended up going far off the narrow road on a [major] tangent to stop ourselves.

So what does that mean for us?

It means we CANNOT walk the narrow road by ourselves.

We CANNOT stay on it by ourselves.

We CANNOT control the dynamics of that walk by ourselves.

We CAN only walk that road, IF we're walking with Papa God by His Spirit.

THE DELUSION OF CONFUSION

Another great way for the enemy to sideline believers is to get them living in confusion.

Confusion in our emotions.

Confusion in our feelings.

Confusion in our thoughts.

Confusion in our beliefs.

Confusion in our experiences.

Confusion in the spiritual.

How does the enemy win? Delude us with confusion. A lot of it. From all sides.

These become anything to keep believers from walking the narrow road with Papa God.

MIXED UNHOLY FIRES

Human Elements Mixed In

Do you remember the mixed unholy fires from *SET THE CAPTIVES*

FREE? Where we saw the unholy mixture of adding human elements into God's pure Truth; and the results that followed.

God does NOT want our human "fragrances" mixed into His Holy Truth—no matter how good we think they smell.

Demonic Elements Mixed In

As we've been seeing in this book, demonic forces are constantly trying to push the Truth of God aside to replace it with their false spirituality. When they cannot succeed fully in pushing God's Truth aside, they gladly settle for mangling the Truth by adding false elements, creating unholy mixtures.

God does NOT want demonic elements mixed into His Holy Truth.

God wants His Holy Fire in us—Unmixed—Pure.

DESENSITIZATION or SENSATIONALISM

Desensitized to the Good

We've become desensitized to the good by being inundated with the broad road and the wide gate of false spiritual Woo. With so much "white noise" in the spiritual air all around us, it becomes harder and harder to see and hear the Truth.

The signal gets lost in the static.

Sensitized to the Bad

Sensationalism is the art of making everything sound urgent, dramatic, or scandalous to get a reaction. One example is where, many times, public media has used common practices to emphasize the dramatic or lurid aspects of events. They present information in an exaggerated way to elicit impassioned reactions.

Sensationalism trades truth for hype, and whatever gets the biggest reaction wins.

Let's be honest. We love sensationalism. In this day and age of video inundation and overstimulation, we want to see the Next Most Exciting thing that keeps our interest for more than ten seconds or we'll move on.

This is where false spiritual Woo works for many. Looking at the many diverse sides of Woo, there are so many potential stimuli to grab their attention that it can easily reach the masses. As mentioned previously, we were all built with the inherent need to find the truth in the spiritual realm because of the need [hole] that God created inside us.

"But I'm not easily deceived! I can tell the difference!"

Can you though?

When you've been swimming in polluted water your whole life, you stop smelling the pollution. When you've been surrounded by spiritual counterfeits since birth, you stop recognizing them as counterfeits.

The fish doesn't know it's wet.

How Desensitization and Sensationalism Work in Us

Course of Events

We start out with childlike faith when we first approach the spiritual—we want to find out who God is and how to fill the empty void inside us. But before we can find the True and Living God, we must recognize that we were raised under the tutelage of the god of this world who rules it.

From the time we were born, the devil has been looking to destroy us—that's his inherent nature—there's **NO** good in him. He set up the environment in the world in which we were raised with the false spiritual Woo all around us. The chips have been stacked against us from the outset. This leads to our loss of innocence.

Therefore, without exception, we **ALL** fall under Woo's spell from the beginning. How much we buy into is a good question. Some may resist. Many will not. The atmosphere of the false spiritual is always around us seeking its next victim.

We eventually become desensitized to God, who created us and wants us to search and find Him, digging through all the garbage laid before us. At the same time, the enemy looks to create sensationalism in anything that might become our Achilles heel. With the over-sensationalized false Woo reaching out to us from every side, we will most likely succumb. We eventually become convinced and believe that we've found the truth, like many other seekers in Woo's counterfeits. And those seekers gather around each other to confirm they've all made the right choice.

Yet God wants us [yearns for us] to return to childlike faith. To seek Him—the One and Only, True and Living God—then we **WILL** find Him; He will be there to show us the way. But that way is narrow. And all the Woo-BS won't fit on that narrow road.

In the second book, I talk about all the tough times in the wilderness **ALL** True Believers **MUST** go through. That's a perfect time for the enemy to tempt us to move away from the Light of God and into the "dark side." Unfortunately, many will fall for this—especially when presented as "light" from the "angels of light."

THE BICYCLE TIRE ANALOGY

Jesus is the Hub in the Center

Picture a bicycle wheel.

The tire on the outside of the wheel is the "broad way" where we live—where "the rubber meets the road." It's full of air—filled by the prince of the power of the air. It's where the good, bad and ugly of the world live, under the ruler of this world. Where all deception lives—and all glitter and false spirituality lives.

We are on the spokes, journeying from many paths and angles to reach the hub—if we're seeking true spirituality in God. All of that is absolutely okay, as long as we're heading in the right direction towards the hub.

As we're heading away from the falseness towards the hub, some will look back at their life on the tire, seeing the glitter and the others they left behind, and will want to return. Some will look to see where others are on their spoke journey as they pass near them. Many will be lured to cross over to someone else's spoke only to retreat up that spoke and go back to their old place of "darkness" with the "angels of light" and false spirituality on the wheel.

God's goal for us is to reach the hub [Jesus] no matter which spoke path, direction, and angle we came from. The enemy's goal it to F— up that process no matter what. No matter how. No matter which way.

"But what if I started on the wrong spoke? What if I went the wrong direction for years?"

Doesn't matter.

Every spoke leads to the hub in the center if you're going in the right direction. The question isn't where you started.

The question is: Which way are you heading now?

THE JOURNEY

Where are you on this journey?

Are you on the tire?

Still living in the broad way, surrounded by the false spiritual, thinking you've found truth in the counterfeits?

Are you on the spokes?

On a journey toward something—but in which direction? Toward the hub or back toward the tire?

If so, going which way?

Are you moving toward Christ or away from Him? Are you getting closer to the narrow gate or further from it?

Have you reached the Hub?

Have you found Jesus—the One and Only Way, Truth, and Life? Are you living IN Christ, walking with Him daily, knowing His voice, following His leading?

THE ROAD IS NARROW

The gate is small.

Few find it.

But it's there. And it's open. And Jesus is standing at it, waiting for you.

The broad road is crowded. It's exciting. It's full of options and experiences and "a truth" that feels so right.

But it leads to destruction.

The narrow road is less popular. It requires surrender. It costs you everything.

But it leads to life.

Choose Wisely.

CHAPTER FOURTEEN

HOW TO CONTROL THE MASSES

THE FIVE WAYS TO CONTROL PEOPLE

ANY OF THE FOLLOWING can be positive, or negative—but all of these areas can have control over our lives. And as you can see, many of these areas will overlap each other.

First: Emotions

We can have good emotions: joy, love, gratitude, compassion, and hope.

We can have bad emotions: anger, fear, sadness, jealousy, and guilt.

Emotions are more immediate than feelings, having instinctive reactions. They're typically more intense, but short-lived, responses to immediate situations or stimuli. These responses are often physiological and automatic.

Emotions can influence our behavior and well-being in various ways. All these emotions can take over and control us.

Second: Feelings

We can have good feelings: contentment, satisfaction, affection, confidence, love, joy, and peace.

We can have bad feelings: anxiety, resentment, frustration, loneliness, regret, hatred, and wrath.

These feelings often reflect how we interpret our emotions and experiences. Feelings are more stable and can last much longer than emotions, and are often influenced by thoughts and experiences developed over time.

Feelings can influence our behavior and well-being in various ways. All these feelings can take over and control us.

Third: Thoughts

We can have good thoughts: optimism, gratitude, compassion, self-compassion, hopefulness, and open-mindedness.

We can have bad thoughts: self-doubt, negativity, fearfulness, jealousy, and worry.

Our minds are full of thoughts. Always coming at us from many directions. Some are good. Some are bad. These thoughts can significantly impact our emotions and behavior—all these thoughts can take over and control us—all influencing us for the better or worse. You can read a lot more about this area in *SET THE CAPTIVES FREE*.

Fourth: Beliefs

We can have good beliefs: the desire to learn and improve, compassion for others, resilience, positivity, integrity, and honesty.

We can have bad beliefs: perfectionism, fear of failure, limiting or negative self-views, cynicism, distrust of others, control over others, victim mentality, and stereotyping.

These beliefs shape our attitudes and behavior in various aspects of life. All our beliefs can take over and control us—all influencing us for the better or worse.

What we believe and our belief systems are deep subjects that deserve much more attention than I'll give them here. Again, you can read a lot more about these areas in *SET THE CAPTIVES FREE*.

Fifth: Experiences

Our life is full of experiences. Once again, some good—some bad.

We can have good experiences: traveling, achievements (personal or professional), meaningful relationships (with friends and family), acts of kindness, and learning new skills (in personal growth and development).

We can have bad experiences: trauma (whether in the emotional, mental or physical), loss and grief (from losing loved ones or things we found important), failure (in disappointments or setbacks), conflict (in arguments or misunderstandings), and betrayal (when let down by someone trusted).

These experiences can significantly shape our perspectives and emotional well-being. All our experiences can take over and control us—all influencing us for the better or worse.

"But Tom, these are just normal human things! What does this have to do with spiritual deception?"

Everything.

Because these are the **Exact Five Levers** the enemy uses to control you. He manipulates your emotions, your feelings, your thoughts, your beliefs, and your experiences—to lead you away from the True and Living God.

He's been doing it since Eden.

And he's very, very good at it.

COUNTERFEITS

As discussed previously, we become convinced that we've found the truth in Woo's counterfeits, as many other seekers have—and we find comfort in that crowd mentality. In convincing each other, we all found the truth. We believe our shared experiences confirm this.

The purveyors of these experiences use them to counter argue against authentic experiences. Simply because these experiences are so much more at the ready. So much more accessible than seeking after the True and Living God, who won't put on a "dog and pony show" for them.

ENCOUNTERS

What if you found out that many things you've come to accept as normal are deceptions?

Maybe not all, but what if most encounters are false?

How would that affect your worldview?

IT'S TIME TO PULL THE CURTAIN BACK

Do you remember in the original "Wizard of Oz" movie when Dorothy's dog, Toto, pulls back the curtain? This action exposed the Great Wizard was only a man standing behind the curtain pulling all the levers.

Now, I'm about to pull back the curtain on Woo and **ALL** the false spiritual to show you the demons behind them pulling the levers. As well as how it's done.

Let's talk about Psychics, Spiritualists, Spirit Guides, Fortune Tellers, and Mediums

Psychics, spiritualists, and fortune tellers are individuals claiming to have abilities to perceive information hidden from the normal senses—often including predictions about the future—or insights into people's lives. And mediums are individuals claiming to have spirit guides with abilities to contact the spirits of the deceased.

Where do these people get these supernatural abilities?

Were they born with gifts?

Are they more tuned in to God than the rest of us?

Actually, they are tuned in to the god of this world and his fallen angels /

demons / spirits. In **THE DAILY STAND** I go into great detail about how these people get their powers and how they "pull off" these charades, facades, pretenses, guises, shows, and masquerades.

Here's an excerpt from **THE DAILY STAND**, which explains how these things work—taken from Chapter Five, *"The Devil is Fifty Feet Tall"*:

Beginning Quote from THE DAILY STAND

HOW DOES HE KNOW WHAT WORKS ON YOU, ME, AND EVERYONE ELSE?

It's pretty simple, really.

As the ruler of this world, he and his demons have been running to and fro across the earth since the beginning of time—observing, gathering info, hoarding data, using it to control not only you but everyone around you.

Just imagine—since the enemy has been doing this for all time, they've gathered ALL information on EVERYONE who's ever lived or died. Consider it the LARGEST COMPUTER DATA BANK on everyone—EVER.

Bigger and more accurate than Google could EVER hope to become, smarter than the most imagined AI machine learning—EVER.

With all that data at their fingertips, can you see why psychics, spiritualists, spirit guides, fortune telling, seances, mystical religions, and the ilk might fool the masses? Accessing data from willing spirits who want to control you.

How about for ghost hunters and such? It's the same for those who go around "sensing" spirits, ghosts of the dead. These spirits can mimic and portray themselves as those ghosts, passing along the same data, using it to create "accurate manifestations."

This backing by the enemy is where these people get their "powers" by connecting and accessing current and past information that will, in turn, cause many to believe in them.

They can very accurately (100 percent) correctly tell you all the current info, whether information about you, those around you, and/or elsewhere, because they're watching over everyone and their every move.

They can very accurately (100 percent) correctly tell you about all the past because they were intimately observing and interacting with those others, including your dead relatives, trying to direct and control them but, no matter what, "documenting" their lives for future use.

Therefore, they can very accurately communicate to you as someone returning to you from "the other side," thereby playing a CON (confidence) GAME on you.

If they can accurately convince you about the current and past, then they can most likely get you under their control.

It's that (potential) 100 percent accuracy that fools most people.

Sidenote: Just another quick tangent. So why did I say "potential?"

You might notice that not all physics, and the ilk, have that "100 percent accurate" rating, reputation, or results—and might use that as an argument against what I'm saying—or at minimum cause you confusion here.

Well, let's go back to the father of lies who's behind all this. In his sadistic twisted mind where he wants to control everybody and everything, he enjoys creating trouble, anxiety, confusion, and competition, even and especially, among his own "followers"—to see who can become the best at becoming his "worst of the worst"—to constantly, more deeply entrap and possess them "forever."

If he gave all those folks, yielding to his evil, instant 100 percent accuracy, then what's the fun in that? He'd rather make them work at it—forcing them to yield to (and worship) him and his (evil) "spirit guides"—making these folks more and more and uber dependent on him and his hordes to achieve their "powers." Therefore, he forces them to compete to "earn" their way up the hierarchy.

Ok, I'm back.

So why do they save telling you the future until last?

Because when they try to predict the future, they're usually only about 50 percent right.

Why? Because they do **NOT** know the future.

They do know the current, so they can tell you all about you and your life or what someone you know might be doing at that moment, anywhere they are in the world, when the "reading" is happening. In such an instance, it seems like they might be telling the (very near) future, but the rest is just a fifty-fifty crap shoot—where they're making logical predictive guessing (like AI today) based on everyone's past histories and their vast "Google-type databases" of human nature reactions to predict future behaviors. Therefore, they will probably be right 50 percent of the time.

They can EASILY DECEIVE THE MASSES when they are 100 percent correct about the current and the past. Then they will be given latitude for only 50 percent accurate future predictions, obtaining people's "buy in" by quoting "everyone has free will" and, therefore, "they might not listen to the spirits trying to guide them in the future."

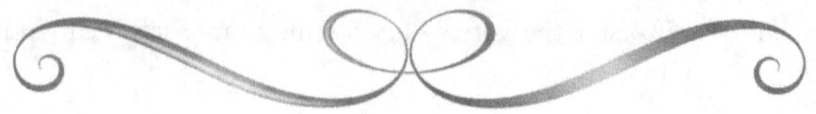

Ending Quote from THE DAILY STAND

"I hear you, Tom, [I'm not really listening...] but listen to me... the psychic knew things nobody else could have known!"

Of course they did.

The demons feeding them information have been watching your entire life. And your parents' lives. And your grandparents' lives. They were there when those conversations happened. They were there when those secrets were shared.

The "accuracy" is the bait.

The hook is what comes after you swallow it.

For great masses, these are captivating deceptions that control them.

How About Ghosts?

Guess I just answered that question in the above excerpt. But let me expand on it a bit more.

Ghosts are not actual entities of dead humans.

They're just demons playing "dress up" to fool the masses.

Which, unfortunately, works on many.

Most everyone "believes in ghosts." Maybe it's our culture we grew up with. Maybe it's experiences we've had or others we trust have told us. Most believe in the spirits of the dead haunting the living. Some, maybe many, have experienced "feelings" or sudden cold, heat, wind, or electricity in a room which had no changes to cause such. Maybe walking into a room, house, graveyard, or elsewhere, to get strange feelings of "a presence." Many have a fear of seeing them or experiencing such presences. While some others have excitement and anticipation to go "find them."

Why the fascination?

Is it fear or excitement about the haunting?

Maybe, some of both. Either way, it's a great deception that controls many.

"But I SAW my grandmother after she died! She appeared to me!"

No, you didn't.

You saw a demon who knew exactly what your grandmother looked like, sounded like, and would say—because they watched her entire life. It knew her mannerisms, her phrases, her secrets.

The dead don't come back to comfort the living.

Demons do.

Wearing the faces of those we loved.

What About Magicians?

Here's another area we open ourselves to without realizing we're giving our control away again.

We love to go see a magic show. If it's just "slight of hand" where we look at the magician's right hand while he/she pulls a trick out with their left hand—that can be innocent.

But what happens when the magician does the "impossible?"

Makes an elephant float in the air?

Makes someone disappear from "here" to reappear "there?"

If it's just an elaborate scheme of hidden ropes, pulleys, hidden doors, etc. then it's explainable in the "slight of hand" venue. But if it's not—no hidden ropes, pulleys, hidden doors, etc.—then where do they get their powers?

If there are only two sources of power as we've clearly discussed to this point—the God of the Universe who won't do "dog and pony shows." Then there's the other source: the god of this world—who will gladly do such and more to gain control over people's thoughts and lives.

What About Mentalists?

Either they have great powers to read people's minds, listen to their thoughts, see what people are writing down, knowing what secrets they're keeping, whispering into another's ears, able to tell you what someone across the world is saying or thinking; or they have an inside secret.

As discussed, they don't have great powers. **NO** human does.

Then what's the inside secret?

Knowingly or unknowingly, they've gained these powers by opening themselves to demonic forces. As they "grew" in their craft, they thought they had tapped into special secret powers—but they didn't.

Let me introduce you to their secret that they may or may not understand. They have at a minimum two familiar spirits working in tandem with them at all times.

We live in a vast unseen spiritual world all around us. Hordes of both angels and demons. If we could see them, it would scare us much more than "believing in" or "seeing" ghosts.

To get a good view of this reality, read the great fictional books by Frank E. Peretti, *"This Present Darkness"* and *"Piercing the Darkness."* They give a great view of the spiritual realm and battles we can't perceive with our natural senses. They show what goes on behind and beyond what our eyes can see or our ears can hear. If you've never read them, I highly recommend you do.

Back to Their Secret:

Let me paint a very simple picture. If you claimed to be a Mentalist and had two assistants working with you that had "invisibility cloaks"—like the "invisible man" or other science fiction movies—with whisper-quiet headsets on.

Yes, I admit it—I enjoy a lot of science fiction.

The first assistant is standing next to you (the Mentalist), ready to whisper into your ear. The second assistant goes out into the crowd [in the same room or on the other side of the world] and looks for a suitable candidate. When they identify that candidate, they whisper through their headset to your assistant, "choose him/her and here's what you need to ask them." So, your assistant relays that info to you, and you proceed: "Sir/Madam what do you want to know? Or would you just like me to tell you what you're thinking about, just wrote down or told your friend?" After they respond, the second assistant relays any additional info to your assistant that you will need while you play the "let me get a reading from your spiritual aura" game—at which time you dazzle that person and the crowd with 100% accuracy of whatever they were thinking, saying or doing.

Wow!

The Mentalist was right! 100% correct.

Oh, they have such great powers!

Or,

If you understood Mentalists are working with two or more familiar spirits (demons) that are on his/her team—whose connections have grown deeply through the years as they yielded to those wrong spirits—who [most likely] do NOT understand the depth of their [WRONG] spiritual connection. And add to this scenario that no one in the natural realm can see nor hear those two assistants—then you'd understand how easy the CON was to pull off.

Again, another great way to control people and what they believe, to draw them into the false spiritual realm.

Angelic Experiences

Remember again, Satan disguises himself [masquerades] as an angel of light:

"And it is no wonder, for Satan himself **disguises (masquerades) as an**

angel of light; So it is not surprising if his servants also **masquerade as ministers of righteousness**." (2 Corinthians 11:14-15)

His servants can be humans, deceived and operating under his control. But his servants are also the one third of the angels that fell with him when he was kicked out of Heaven. Those spirits also masquerade as angels of light.

Does that leave room in your thoughts to understand that many, many angelic encounters might be with these demons?

It should.

Because many are.

How easy to fool God's people, as well as many others in the world, to follow the wrong spiritual forces.

How can we distinguish the difference between God's real angels and the fallen demonic ones who dress up as "light?"

First and foremost, we must learn how to distinguish the voices that are from God and His angels versus all the wrong voices. Again, I will remind you to go back and reread *SET THE CAPTIVES FREE* to learn how you can truly distinguish between the right and wrong voices to know with unquestionable assurity.

But for now, here are a few dead giveaways to demonic angels of light.

If the angel is directing you to anything short of worshipping the One and Only, True and Living God, **IT'S FALSE**.

If the angel is promising "blessings," riches, power, or similar, **IT'S FALSE**. Like all the angel crap running over social media feeds nowadays saying things like "repeat these numbers," "play these numbers," "do 'this or that'," and you'll get rich or receive a GREAT blessing. **It's pure BS**.

If the angel is promoting anything that would build up your pride, your self or promoting you having some great purpose or ministry or abilities to heal or do anything that doesn't humble you under the hand of the Only True God, **IT'S FALSE**.

If the angel is directing you to anything short of humbling yourself under and to the One and Only, True and Living God, **IT'S FALSE**.

The list could probably go on "forever." It's time for God's children to learn His voice over all others.

Spiritual Beings

What about any other spiritual beings other than angels that appear to people?

Are they any different from the false angels?

NO.

Once again, they're fallen angels / demons / spirits putting on disguises. Anything to fool the masses. And unfortunately, they do their job well.

Aliens

Personally, I don't know if there's life on other planets and if some encounters people have had are with aliens traveling here from other planets. I'm not smart enough to prove that one way or the other.

I know this will be controversial to many. But I believe that most alien encounters are demons playing "dress up" again.

You might think I'm crazy.

If so, join the crowd.

But over the years, with all the evidence I've seen and experienced watching the curtain being pulled back on the work of the enemy, over and over again, I'm convinced most alien encounters are demons. While we normally cannot see spirits nor the spiritual realm, they can appear to us in many human forms, if and when they want us to see them. Whether that's as "angels," "ghosts," "other spiritual beings," "a presence", sensations, electricity in the air, or outright demonic attacks.

So why not aliens?

How simple of a way to fool the masses again.

And yes, since spirits can fly as well as take on forms and appearances of most anything on earth, then why not think they're transforming into the "spaceships" and "flying saucers" seen flying, darting back and forth at uncontrollable speeds [from human terms] in the skies.

I've not experienced being "abducted by aliens," but over the many years I've dealt with many demonic presences, forces, beings, and their BS. One thing some have reported is that after being "abducted" they called out on the name of Jesus and the "aliens" left them alone instantly.

This I can attest to: when I've called out on the Lord Jesus during the many times when the enemy was pulling their BS on me, they and their presence dissipated immediately. To learn more about this, as well as us having "all authority over all the enemy" (Luke 10:17-20), read more in ***THE DAILY STAND***.

Spiritual Other...

Many types. Many ways.

Whether it's through the paranormal, astrology, the many spiritual-type cards, idols, crystals, etc. or powers, altars, sacrifices, spells, and incantations, it's all part of the great rouse being played on the masses by the god of this world and his demon cohorts.

Laughing their asses off at the gullibility and ignorance of the fallen human race.

So am I saying that all strange presences, appearances, apparitions, feelings, waves, hot, cold, dreams, visions, depressions, fears, anxiety, hate, anger, wrath—many with immediate emotions and "off strange feelings" are always demonic?

What about sudden headaches, pain, sickness, etc.? Or strange smells, strange lights or strange anything coming out of the blue? Are they always demonic?

No, not all are demonic.

Things can just be mental, emotional, physiological, or psychological challenges happening in our lives. But you need to remember we were raised in this world under the tutelage of the god of this world and his cohorts. So, keeping this in mind, we need to understand we've been trained as mice running his mazes; and those challenges may still have come from demonic influence.

But for those things that come on you suddenly and out of the blue.

A whole heck of a lot of them are.

What about "possessed" objects?

Many believe that there are "possessed dolls" or other "possessed objects" that they've encountered, heard of or at minimum seen on TV and in the movies. I hate to burst your bubble [actually, I don't mind], but NONE /

ZERO / NADA are any type of living entities.

You mean there aren't really "possessed dolls" or other objects doing evil?

NO there aren't.

Just evil doing evil through them. Just objects with demons attached to and/or manipulating through the objects for every ill effect possible on the gullible and misinformed.

IF OUR EYES WERE OPENED

If we could only see what's behind the curtain on ALL these things.

Demons pulling the levers controlling the masses.

IF WE ONLY KNEW

If we ONLY understood the Truth.

We'd NEVER be or respond the same to

any of this.

EVER again.

LEAVE A REVIEW

HOW WOULD YOU REVIEW SET THE CAPTIVES FREE TOO?

Scan to Review

How did the book affect you?

Have you been set free, are you being set free, or do you know someone who needs to be?

Be honest with yourself and review accordingly so others can be set free as well.

Thank you for reading and reviewing SET THE CAPTIVES FREE TOO.   – Tom

CHAPTER FIFTEEN

PREMISE OF TRUTH

THE TRUE SPIRITUAL

EVERYTHING IN THIS BOOK HINGES ON ONE QUESTION:

Is there such a thing as Absolute Truth?

I F THERE IS, THEN everything I've written matters. If there isn't, then nothing matters—not this book, not your beliefs, not your experiences, not your life.

So let's establish the premise.

IF ONLY TWO SOURCES OF POWER

We've established throughout this book that there are only two sources of spiritual power in the universe:

1. **The One and Only, True and Living God**—Creator of Heaven and Earth, Father of Jesus Christ, the Great **I AM**.

2. **The god of this world**—Satan, the devil, the enemy, the father of lies, and his fallen angels / demons / spirits.

That's it. Two. Not three. Not seven. Not a million.

Two.

"But Tom, that's so binary! So black and white! The universe is more complex than that!"

Is it though?

Light or darkness. Life or death. Truth or lies. Good or evil.

The enemy loves complexity. He loves gray areas. He loves "nuance" and "spectrum" and "it depends." Because in the gray, he can hide. In the complexity, he can confuse. In the "nuance," he can deceive.

In the spiritual realm, there are no "50 shades of gray."

God is simple—He is: I AM.

Then God is ONE and His Word is TRUE

If there are only two sources, and one is the Creator of everything, then:

God is **ONE**—not many gods, not a pantheon, not "the universe," not "source energy," not "higher consciousness." One God. One Creator. One Authority.

His Word is **TRUE**—not partially true, not "containing truth," not "inspired but fallible," not "one of many sacred texts." True. Completely. Absolutely. Without error in its original form.

This is the foundation. This is the premise. Without this, everything crumbles.

Then All Else is Bunched Together and FALSE

Here's where it gets uncomfortable for a lot of people.

If there are only two sources of spiritual power, and God is the source of all Truth, then **everything else** —no matter how it's packaged, no matter what it's called, no matter how "spiritual" it feels—comes from the **other source**.

Hinduism, Buddhism, Islam, New Age, Wicca, Spiritualism, Mysticism, Quantum Consciousness, Law of Attraction, Manifestation, Energy Healing, Psychic Powers, Channeling, Astrology, Tarot, Crystals, Chakras, Reiki, Transcendental Meditation, Yoga philosophy, Kabbalah, Sufism, Shamanism, Animism, Ancestor Worship...

ALL bunched together.

ALL from the same source.

ALL false.

"That's incredibly offensive! How dare you lump all those traditions together! Some of them are ancient! Some of them have helped millions of people!"

I'm not saying they're not ancient. I'm not saying people haven't had experiences. I'm not saying they may've "helped" some people.

I'm saying the source is the same.

The enemy has had thousands of years to develop thousands of counterfeits. He's not stupid. He customizes the deception for every culture, every era, every personality type. Hindu mysticism for the East. New Age for the West. Prosperity gospel for the materialistic. Social justice spirituality for the activists. Quantum Woo for the intellectuals.

Different packaging.

Same source.

Same destination.

COMPARE TRUE SPIRITUAL

Let's compare the True spiritual from God versus the fake from the enemy.

True Spiritual (From God)

Source: The One and Only, True and Living God—Father, Son, Holy Spirit.

Access: Through Jesus Christ alone. "I am THE Way, THE Truth, and THE Life. No one comes to the Father except through Me." (John 14:6)

Foundation: Scripture—the written Word of God. Objective. External. Unchanging.

Method: Faith in Christ, surrender to God, obedience to His Word, led by His Spirit.

Goal: Relationship with God, transformation into Christ's image, eternal life with Him.

Fruit: Love, joy, peace, patience, kindness, goodness, faithfulness, gentleness, self-control. (Galatians 5:22-23)

Cost: Everything. Death to self. Complete surrender. "Whoever wants to save their life will lose it, but whoever loses their life for me will find it." (Matthew 16:25)

False Spiritual (From the Enemy)

Source: The god of this world—Satan and his demons, masquerading as light, wisdom, enlightenment.

Access: Many paths. "All roads lead to the same place." "Find your own truth." "Whatever works for you."

Foundation: Experience, feelings, inner knowing, "resonance." Subjective. Internal. Ever-changing.

Method: Techniques, practices, rituals, altered states, meditation, visualization, energy work, awakening.

Goal: Self-improvement, enlightenment, higher consciousness, power, manifestation, becoming "god."

Fruit: Pride, self-focus, spiritual experiences without transformation, bondage disguised as freedom.

Cost: Your soul. But they don't tell you that upfront.

THE KEY DIFFERENCES

Direction

True spiritual: Points away from self, toward God. Humbles you. Decreases you. Increases Him.

False spiritual: Points toward self, away from God. Elevates you. Increases you. Decreases Him (or eliminates Him entirely).

Authority

True spiritual: God's Word is the authority. You submit to it. You don't get to reinterpret it to fit your preferences.

False spiritual: You are the authority. Your experience. Your feelings. Your "inner knowing." You decide what's true for you.

Exclusivity

True spiritual: Exclusive. One way. Narrow gate. "No one comes to the Father except through Me."

False spiritual: Inclusive. Many ways. Wide gate. "All paths lead to the same destination."

EGO'S PLACE IN THE MIX

Here's where it gets really interesting.

False spirituality often talks about "killing the ego" or "transcending the ego." Sounds humble, right? Sounds like it's pointing away from self.

But watch what actually happens.

In false spirituality, YOU are the one doing the work. YOU are achieving enlightenment. YOU are raising your consciousness. YOU are becoming awakened. YOU are manifesting your reality. YOU are discovering the god within.

Even when they talk about "ego death," it's still all about **YOU**.

"But Christianity talks about transformation too! What's the difference?"

The difference is WHO does the work.

In true spirituality, **GOD** does the work. You surrender. You submit. You yield. And HE transforms you. It's not your achievement—it's His grace. Not your effort—His power. Not your awakening—His revelation.

"I have been crucified with Christ. It is no longer I who live, but Christ who lives in me." (Galatians 2:20)

That's the difference

In false spirituality, you become more.

In true spirituality, you become less—and He becomes everything.

WHY GOOD PEOPLE FALL FOR THE FALSE

So why do people fall for the counterfeit? Why do intelligent, sincere, seeking people end up in false spirituality?

1. It Appeals to Pride

"You can become enlightened." "You have the power within." "You are already divine." "You can manifest your reality." "You are enough."

This is the original lie from the Garden: "You will be like God."

And we still fall for it because our egos love to hear it.

2. It Avoids Surrender

False spirituality lets you stay in control. You pick your practices. You choose your beliefs. You determine your truth. You don't have to submit to anyone or anything outside yourself.

True spirituality requires complete surrender to a God who gets to tell you what's true, what's right, and how to live.

That's terrifying to the ego.

3. It Offers Experiences

The enemy is happy to provide spiritual experiences. Feelings of peace. Sensations of energy. Visions. Encounters. Manifestations. Signs and wonders.

God doesn't do "dog and pony shows" on demand.

The enemy will—because experiences are his hook.

4. It Sounds Loving

"All paths lead to God." "Everyone is saved." "Love is love." "Don't judge." "Accept everyone's truth."

Sounds so inclusive. So accepting. So loving. But a doctor who tells you that you're fine when you have stage-4 cancer and don't need treatment of any kind isn't loving—he's sentencing you to death.

Truth that saves is more loving than lies that comfort.

5. The Bible Has Been Attacked

For centuries, the enemy has worked to undermine confidence in Scripture. "It's been translated too many times." "It's full of contradictions." "It was written by men." "It's outdated." "It's been used to oppress people."

If he can get you to doubt the Word, he can get you to accept anything else.

CONVINCING THOSE WHO'VE BEEN DECEIVED

So how do you convince someone who's been deceived that they are deceived?

Honestly?

You often can't.

Not with arguments. Not with evidence. Not with logic.

"Then why write this book?"

Because some will have ears to hear. Because the Holy Spirit can use Truth to break through deception. Because seeds planted today may bear fruit years from now.

Because even if ONE person is set free, IT'S WORTH IT!

The arguments from the deceived usually sound like this:

"The Bible is fallible." — Then you have no objective standard for truth, and everything is just opinion.

"There are many sources of spiritual power." — Name one that doesn't ultimately trace back to either God or the enemy.

"My experience tells me otherwise." — The enemy can provide experiences. **Feelings aren't Truth.**

"That's your truth, not mine." — Truth isn't "yours" or "mine." It's Truth. It exists independently of our opinions about it.

"A loving God wouldn't be so exclusive." — A loving God already provided **ONE way** that **actually works** rather than letting everyone wander into destruction.

THE PREMISE STANDS

Here's the premise of truth:

There are only two sources of spiritual power.

God is One, and His Word **is TRUE.**

Everything else—no matter what it's called, how it's packaged, or how it feels—is from the other source and is **FALSE.**

You can accept this premise or reject it.

But you can't escape the consequences of your choice.

The narrow road is narrow for a reason.

The broad road is broad for a reason.

CHOOSE WISELY.

CHAPTER SIXTEEN

THE PATH TO FREEDOM

FREEDOM IS POSSIBLE

N O MATTER HOW DEEP you've gone. No matter how long you've been involved. No matter how "gifted" you think you are. No matter how many spiritual experiences you've had. Freedom is possible through Jesus Christ.

The same name that raised Jesus from the dead was given to break every chain of spiritual bondage and set the captives free.

This chapter provides a comprehensive, step-by-step process for breaking free from all forms of spiritual deception. While each person's journey is unique, these principles apply universally and have been proven effective in countless lives.

Remember, you are not alone in this process. Papa God's heart breaks for His children trapped in deception, and He's actively working to bring you into the Light of His Truth and Love.

"But Tom, I've been doing this for years! It's part of who I am!"

No, it isn't.

It's part of what you've been deceived into thinking you are. There's a difference. Your true identity is found in Christ—not in spiritual practices, not in experiences, not in "gifts" that came from the wrong source.

Let's get you free.

UNDERSTANDING SPIRITUAL BONDAGE

The Nature of Spiritual Bondage

Spiritual bondage rarely happens overnight.

It typically develops through: Initial curiosity as innocent exploration of spiritual topics. Gradual involvement as increasing participation in deceptive practices. Experiential validation of supernatural experiences that seem to confirm the practices. Identity integration makes these practices central to personal identity. Defensive protection in defending the practices when challenged. And complete immersion in a new total lifestyle and worldview based on deception.

The Components of Spiritual Bondage

Mental Bondage: Thought patterns programmed by deceptive teaching. Confusion about spiritual truth and reality. Inability to think clearly about spiritual matters. Mental oppression and confusion.

Emotional Bondage: Fear of leaving familiar spiritual practices. Guilt and shame from past involvement. Anger toward those who challenge the deception. Emotional dependence on spiritual experiences.

Spiritual Bondage: Actual demonic influence, oppression, and possession. Spiritual contracts and agreements made with entities. Curses and spiritual attacks from involvement. Separation from an authentic relationship with God.

Social Bondage: Relationships built around deceptive practices. Identity tied to spiritual community involvement. Fear of rejection from spiritual friends and family. Financial investment in deceptive practices and training.

RECOGNITION AND AWAKENING

Spiritual Eye Opening

"The god of this world has blinded the minds of the unbelievers." (2 Corinthians 4:4)

Before anyone can be free, they must first see their bondage. This requires honest self-assessment.

Your reality check questions:

Am I truly free, or just convinced that I am?

Do I experience increasing spiritual confusion or clarity?

Do my spiritual practices bring lasting peace and freedom?

Can I easily walk away from these practices without distress?

Do I defend these practices when challenged from Scripture?

Am I becoming more humble or more spiritually proud?

Has my involvement led me closer to or further from biblical Christianity?

Do I have **THE PEACE** that passes understanding or anxiety about spiritual performance?

"But my practices have helped me so much! I feel more peaceful, more connected, more spiritual!"

Feelings aren't Truth.

The enemy can provide feelings of "peace." He can provide experiences of "connection." He can make you feel very "spiritual."

That's his specialty—counterfeits that feel real.

The question isn't how it feels. The question is: What does Scripture say?

Becoming exposed to the Truth:

Study what Scripture actually says about these spiritual practices. Research the historical and spiritual roots of your practices. Read about and listen to the testimonies of others who have found freedom from these same things, as Morgane Rose told you in Chapter One. And ask God to show you the truth about your spiritual condition.

Counting the Cost

"Which of you, desiring to build a tower, does not first sit down and count the cost?" (Luke 14:28)

Freedom often requires significant sacrifice. Be prepared for:

Relationship Costs: You will need to leave spiritual communities and groups. Some spiritual friends may reject you. Family members involved in deception may oppose your freedom. Spiritual mentors and teachers will likely try to stop you.

Financial Costs: Money spent on training, books, and materials will be lost. Income from spiritual services or teaching will end. Investment in spiritual education may seem wasted. Lifestyle changes may be financially challenging.

Identity Costs: Spiritual identity and sense of specialness will disappear. Feeling of spiritual advancement and superiority will end. Certainty about spiritual gifts and calling will be questioned. Public reputation as a spiritual person may be damaged.

Emotional Costs: Grief over lost spiritual experiences and relationships. Shame about having been deceived for so long. Fear about the unknown path ahead. Anger at those who led you into deception.

Deciding

Freedom requires a definitive decision, not just wishful thinking.

The Commitment: "I choose to pursue biblical Truth over my current spiritual practices, regardless of the cost."

The Surrender: "I surrender my need to understand everything and trust God to lead me into truth."

The Humility: "I acknowledge that I have been deceived and need God's help to find truth."

CONFESSION AND REPENTANCE

Thorough Confession

"If we confess our sins, he is faithful and just to forgive us our sins and to cleanse us from all unrighteousness." (1 John 1:9)

True confession involves specific acknowledgment of spiritual rebellion:

Confess the root sin:

"I confess that I have sought spiritual power, wisdom, and experience from sources other than You, God."

"I acknowledge that this represents rebellion against Your authority and desire to be my own god."

"I admit that I have been spiritually prideful and believed lies about my spiritual condition."

Confess specific practices: Make a detailed list of every spiritual practice you've been involved in. Whether it's energy healing, Reiki, chakra work, manifestation, Law of Attraction, vision boards, meditation practices that empty the mind or invoke entities, yoga with spiritual components, crystal healing, sage burning, spiritual cleansing, Tarot cards, astrology, psychic readings, shamanic practices, plant medicine, spirit guides or any form of divination and fortune-telling or any other mentioned so far or not.

Confess the fruit of your involvement: Spiritual pride and a sense of superiority. Judgment of biblical Christians as "less enlightened." Leading others into deceptive practices. Defending deception when challenged.

Genuine Repentance

Genuine repentance is ONLY accomplished after asking the Lord to come into our lives. ONLY then can we yield ourselves to the Holy Spirit and have a deep, true repentance to the Lord. It's an attitude of the heart and mind where we choose to turn 180 degrees away from our sins and turn towards God.

The simple truth from God's point of view is that genuine repentance is simply a choice, then asking Him to forgive us and separate the sin in our lives as far as the east is from the west.

"God's kindness is meant to lead you to repentance." (Romans 2:4)

"Those whom I love, I reprove and discipline, so be zealous and repent." (Revelation 3:19)

"God commands all people everywhere to repent." (Acts 17:30)

"Unless you repent, you will all likewise perish." (Luke 13:3)

"Repent therefore, and turn back, that your sins may be blotted out." (Acts 3:19)

Then...

"You (the Lord) will cast ALL our sins into the depths of the sea." (Micah 7:19)

"I, even I, am He who blots out your transgressions...and remembers your sins no more." (Isaiah 43:25)

"I will forgive their wickedness and will remember their sins no more." (Hebrews 8:12)

And...

"As far as the east is from the west, so far has He removed our transgressions from us." (Psalms 103:12)

Repentance goes beyond confession involving a complete change of mind and direction. Then, actions will follow. This is not legalism, but part of a relationship with Him.

Mental repentance: Acknowledging that these practices are spiritually dangerous regardless of how they feel. Accepting that Scripture is the final authority on spiritual Truth. Embracing humility about your spiritual knowledge and experience. Then, choosing to trust God's wisdom over your own understanding.

Emotional repentance: [This is a normal part of the grieving process.] Feeling genuine sorrow for rebelling against God's authority. Grieving the time wasted in spiritual deception. Expressing heartbreak over leading others into deception. Then rejoicing in God's mercy and forgiveness.

Behavioral repentance: Immediately stopping **ALL** involvement in deceptive spiritual practices. Removing **ALL** materials and objects related to these practices. Ending relationships that are based on shared deception. Begin studying Scripture and building biblical spiritual practices.

RENUNCIATION AND BREAKING AGREEMENTS

Specific Renunciation

"They broke down the sacred pillars and cut down the wooden images." (2 Chronicles 34:3-4)

Renunciation involves formally breaking ties with spiritual deception.

Make a comprehensive renunciation list for yourself:

All forms of energy healing and manipulation.

Every manifestation and reality creation technique.

All meditation practices that don't focus on Scripture.

Any spiritual practices borrowed from non-Christian religions.

All divination and fortune-telling methods.

Every spiritual teacher, guru, or guide who led you into deception.

All spiritual communities and organizations promoting deception.

And anything else you can think of as discussed to this point.

Then, by verbal renunciation. Speak aloud:

"Standing in the name of Jesus, alone, I turn away and renounce ALL involvement with [each specific practice you did from your list]. I give myself over to the Spirit of God and allow Him to have full rights in and around me, my family and ALL I have. I declare that I no longer give any spiritual entity the right to influence my life through any of these practices in any way, directly or indirectly. By the blood of Jesus, I bind up, break and cut off any and all spiritual contracts or agreements I have made, whether knowingly or unknowingly. I give the Holy Spirit permission to fill in and around me forever. This I do as I yield myself to You, Lord, alone, and no other spirits ever again."

Breaking Soul Ties and Spiritual Contracts

Spiritual deception often involves actual spiritual agreements that must be broken.

You need to identify any spiritual contracts you made:

Formal initiations into spiritual traditions.

Vows or commitments made to spiritual teachers.

Agreements with spirit guides or entities.

Dedications of yourself or your gifts to spiritual purposes.

Knowingly or unknowingly asking or allowing spirits to come into or around your life.

As well as financial or time commitments to deceptive organizations.

All these things can not only allow spiritual oppression or possession, but create strong "soul ties" to people, things, traditions and more. You can learn much more about these subjects in ***THE DAILY STAND***.

Continuing on from the verbal renunciation above, to break these soul ties and agreements, say:

"As I yield myself to the Lord and stand in the blood of Jesus, I break every spiritual contract and agreement I have made with [name ALL specific entities, teachers or organizations]. I declare these agreements null and void in Jesus' name. I reclaim any spiritual ground I gave away through these agreements and dedicate myself entirely to Jesus Christ, alone. I loose the Holy Spirit to come fill in and around me, my family, my household and all I have."

GETTING TO A PLACE OF "PEACE BE STILL"

Many people involved in spiritual deception have actual demonic oppression and possession that must be addressed—not necessarily at this moment—but down the road in the near future. You may have a long journey ahead of you to get fully released and restored in your heart and mind. **This is normal.** It's going to take a while, but **this journey will be more than worth it** to be fully free and learn to live in the Presence and walk with Papa God.

You should read *THE DAILY STAND* to learn more about these subjects and then get help from competent leaders, believers, and in churches that teach true freedom in the Lord. Ask the Holy Spirit to lead you to competent people who can teach, train, and help you. Read *SET THE CAPTIVES FREE* to help navigate your way through the wrong bodies of believers and find the correct ones that yield themselves to the Lord, who will help build you up—versus putting false belief systems on you, trying to rule over you. The Holy Spirit is more than capable of doing this for you as you will learn from *THE DAILY STAND* in how to walk in **THE PEACE** of God that passes understanding and comprehension.

Until then, you can pray: "I yield myself completely to Jesus and the Holy Spirit. And by the blood of Jesus, I bind up and command every unclean spirit that has gained access to my life through spiritual deception to Be Still [quiet] NOW. You no longer have legal rights to influence me because I'm under the blood of Jesus. I have confessed my sin, renounced these practices, and broken all agreements. I loose the Holy Spirit to take over, in and around me, so Stop and Be Still."

A CRITICAL WARNING ABOUT DELIVERANCE

I need to take a few minutes here to distinguish a very important difference in the subject of deliverance. A lot of good believers are convinced that they're supposed to be in the deliverance ministry. Actually, if they're walking with the Father as Jesus walked, then they are—but just not the way most of them think.

People confuse the word deliverance with being equal to the act of casting out demons. That's not correct. Deliverance is actually more about 'yasha' [in the Hebrew]—which means to "save" or "deliver," 'natsal' [in the Hebrew]—which means to "deliver" or "rescue," or in the Greek 'soteria'—which means "salvation" or "deliverance" and 'rhuomai'—which also means to "deliver" or "rescue."

Going back to one of the original scriptures about Jesus setting the captives free: "The Spirit of the Lord is upon Me, because He hath anointed Me to preach the gospel to the poor; He hath sent Me to heal the brokenhearted, to preach **DELIVERANCE** [or **RELEASE**] *to the Captives*, and recovering of sight to the blind, to set at liberty them that are bruised." (Luke 4:18 KJV)

The word "deliverance" used here is the Greek word 'aphesis', which means "dismissal," "release," "pardon," or "forgiveness."

Therefore, what deliverance really means

Is being **SET FREE**, released, pardoned, dismissed, and forgiven **from captivity**—no matter what kind.

Could that include demon possession?

Yes, but that's NOT Primary, nor First.

The most common Greek words when Jesus and the disciples cast out demons are 'ekballo'—which means "to cast out" and 'exerchomai'—which means "to come out." So, while "deliverance" words can refer to "freedom from evil" generally; the specific act of casting out demons uses different vocabulary in the original texts. Because they are different.

They need to be understood differently.

They need to operate separately.

Understand, while you may need some demons cast out of you or from around you type-of-deliverance someday, don't make that a primary focus for yourself at all.

"But I've read books about deliverance! I've seen videos! Can't I just cast these things out myself?"

I'm telling you as someone who's been around the block, many times over the last 55+ years, walking with Papa God—**this is not a subject to be taken lightly**.

And no matter what you read or heard otherwise, **NEVER** do any such "self-deliverance" nor let anyone rush you into any such kind of deliverance, for a while—maybe a long while. That type of deliverance is nothing to play with nor to rush into. Unfortunately, many do—many want the "crap removed" from within and/or around them ASAP. And unfortunately, many books, many preachers and teachers are pushing this as "the right thing" to do.

Again, as someone who's been with the Lord for a long time—do not be in a RUSH. You can trust the Holy Spirit to do the correct things at the correct time—if you'll yield to Him alone.

While I teach a lot about spiritual warfare in *THE DAILY STAND*, I also warn about the misuse of such deliverance.

You really need to read my first two books to understand why Jesus told us, "When an impure spirit comes out of a person, it goes through arid (waterless) places seeking rest, and does not find it. Then it says, 'I will return to the house I left.' When it arrives, it finds the house swept clean, and put in order. Then it goes and takes seven other spirits, more wicked than itself, and they go in, and live there. And, **the FINAL CONDITION of that person is WORSE than the FIRST**." (Luke 11:24–26)

In **THE DAILY STAND** I continue this area by teaching about the backfilling of the Holy Spirit. If that doesn't happen correctly, as a permanent solution, and the house is found "swept clean", then "**the FINAL CONDITION**" of that person will become "**WORSE than the FIRST**." Why? Because the original demon plus seven other spirits "more wicked than itself" are given **FULL PERMISSION** to come refill that empty house—making the condition of the person **EIGHT TIMES WORSE**. No wonder Jesus gave us the warning.

CLEANSING AND REMOVAL

Spiritual Cleansing

There will be many spiritual areas that require cleansing—some might require the type of deliverance stated above—but as said, do **NOT** be in a rush. God has His perfect timing for you. Allow the Holy Spirit to direct **ALL** your paths. He will lead you into the Truth as you need it. Study the Scriptures. Learn God's Word. And let **THE PEACE** rule.

Some things may never require any kind of external deliverance. These will be the other types of deliverance: being set free, released, pardoned, dismissed, and forgiven from captivity. Pertaining to areas in your life that the Holy Spirit will identify and then transform you—as He changes you from the inside out.

When moving forward with the Spirit of God, don't be surprised at the things that will need to be changed. With His help to close doors you had opened:

Spirits of deception and confusion.

Religious spirits and false spirituality.

Spirits of pride and spiritual superiority.

Familiar spirits posing as guides or angels.

Spirits of fear and spiritual bondage.

Physical Cleansing

"Many of those who were now believers came, confessing and divulging their practices. And a number of those who had practiced magic arts brought their books together and burned them in the sight of all." (Acts 19:18-19)

Physical objects can hold spiritual significance, allowing demonic entities to attach themselves to them. Therefore, they **MUST** be removed and destroyed. Such as, **ALL** books teaching spiritual deception. Crystals, stones, and healing objects. Spiritual jewelry and symbols. Sage, incense, and cleansing materials used in rituals. Tarot cards, oracle cards, and divination tools. Spiritual artwork and statues. Essential oils used for spiritual purposes. And music that promotes deceptive spirituality.

How to remove them:

Do not sell or give them away (this spreads the deception to someone else).

Destroy them completely.

Burn if possible; otherwise, throw away.

Pray over your living space after removal.

Ask God to cleanse your environment of spiritual influences.

Study *THE DAILY STAND* to learn how to do these things and more.

Digital and Media Cleansing

Modern spiritual deception often involves digital content that needs removal:

Apps for meditation, manifestation, or spiritual guidance.

Social media follows of spiritual teachers promoting deception.

YouTube and other channel subscriptions teaching New Age concepts or other covered subjects.

Podcast subscriptions promoting spiritual deception.

Online courses and memberships in deceptive spiritual programs.

Digital books and materials stored on devices.

This will include online presence cleanup:

Remove posts promoting spiritual deception from your social media. Then leave ALL groups that have anything to do with spiritual deception.

Unsubscribe from email lists of deceptive spiritual teachers.

Cancel memberships in spiritual communities and organizations.

Delete profiles on spiritual networking sites.

Remove spiritual services listings if you were a practitioner.

And remove all email, texting and/or other contacts to spiritual connection people who have not chosen to move away from Woo and towards the Lord along with you.

REPLACEMENT AND RENEWAL

Filling the Spiritual Vacuum

As stated above, "When the unclean spirit has gone out of a person, it passes through waterless places seeking rest, and finding none it says, **'I will return to my house from which I came'**." Nature abhors a vacuum—both in the physical and spiritual. You must replace deceptive practices with the Holy Spirit and biblical truth.

Study the Bible deeply and memorize the Scriptures. Begin with basic salvation passages (Romans 3:23-24, 6:23, 10:9-10). Study the Gospel of John to understand Jesus' identity—but return to Matthew to study all the Gospels. As you continue to learn, memorize verses that counter specific deceptions you believed.

Ask the Holy Spirit to guide you, by **His PEACE** that passes understanding, to find a good local small group of believers and a church to grow in. Join a Bible study group focused on foundational Christian doctrine. Study my first two books. They're not quick reads. If you treat them like that, you'll miss the main points.

Develop a real, true, and active daily prayer life with the Father—this is vital to your success. Learn that praying to the Father is **NOT** rote and should never become such. It's **NOT** a set of things to repeat that someone taught you. It's an actual relationship with the One True God who spoke the world into being—that wants this personal relationship with you more than you do.

You should practice thanksgiving and praise instead of demanding or expecting instant answers, as you were wrongly taught in "manifestation." Develop intercessory prayer for others instead of focusing on personal desires. Learn to surrender your will to God's will in prayer.

In terms of Christian fellowship. Find a biblically sound church committed to Scripture, not pushing false belief systems as explained in *SET THE CAPTIVES FREE*. Develop relationships with mature believers who can help keep you accountable to God—not men. Be honest about your past involvement and need for spiritual guidance. Avoid churches that mix biblical truth with New Age or any false spiritual concepts.

Develop good biblical spiritual practices such as worship and praise focused on God's character and works. Meditate on Scripture rather than emptying your mind. Make non-religious prayer—talking to the Father in the most casual way as a best friend—part of your daily life. Continue practicing daily biblical confession and repentance rather than positive affirmations.

Renewing Your Mind

"Do not be conformed to this world, but be transformed by the renewal of your mind." (Romans 12:2)

Your mind has been programmed with deceptive thinking patterns that must be renewed.

It becomes vitally important to identify deceptive thought patterns you most likely learned and now must be unlearned. Such as: "I can control my circumstances through spiritual techniques," "I am a divine being with unlimited potential," "My spiritual experiences validate my beliefs," "Biblical Christians are less spiritually evolved," and "I can create my own spiritual truth."

These things need to be replaced with Biblical Truth. Such as: "God is sovereign over all circumstances, and I trust His perfect will," "I am God's beloved child, created in His image but not divine myself," "Scripture, backed by **THE PEACE**, are the standards for evaluating all spiritual experiences," "Humble submission to biblical truth is true spiritual maturity," and "God has revealed Truth through His Word, and I submit to His authority alone."

Some daily mind renewal practices:

Prayer: Start each day by praying directly to the Father. Remember this is a relationship, not rote. You don't need to act "religious" or "fake spiritual", clasp your hands, get on your knees—none of which impress God, the Father.

Read: Try reading Scripture during the day—but don't let yourself feel guilty if it doesn't always work out—life happens.

Practice: Take every thought captive (2 Corinthians 10:3-5) when deceptive ideas arise.

Use: Scriptural affirmations rather than New Age declarations.

And, **End Each Day**: Reviewing God's faithfulness rather than your spiritual performance.

HEALING AND RESTORATION

Emotional and Psychological Healing

Freedom from spiritual deception often reveals underlying wounds that were the root causes for moving into deception and therefore need healing.

Some common emotional issues are anger, hate, wrath, and unforgiveness for the many possible traumas you may've experienced in your life. Including sexual abuse, mental abuse, physical abuse, leadership and church abuse. And many other possible traumas not named here—each one knows their own they've lived through. These areas will need to be addressed specifically down the road so that you can receive healing for each. That's far beyond the scope of this book, but must be understood as doorways that may've led you into seeking answers in spiritual deception.

Additionally, after making the decision to move beyond the spiritual deceptions, there will be other emotional areas you may need to address, such as grief over lost relationships and investments. Fear of the future without familiar spiritual practices. Depression as spiritual-high experiences fade. Anger toward those who led you into deception. And shame about having been deceived for so long.

How to start the approach towards healing:

Acknowledge these emotions as normal parts of the healing process.

Bring all feelings to God in honest prayer.

Seek biblical counseling from trained Christian counselors that you've vetted first.

Find (vetted) support groups for people recovering from spiritual deception.

Practice forgiveness toward those who deceived you.

Avoiding ungodly healing methods:

Do not return to energy healing or alternative spiritual therapies.

Avoid counselors who mix psychology with New Age concepts.

Be cautious of "Christian" therapists who use ungodly methods—vet them first.

Do not seek healing through continued spiritual experiences.

Rebuilding Spiritual Identity

Your identity was likely tied to your spiritual practices and must be rebuilt on a proper biblical foundation.

False identity elements to release:

Such as, identity as a "spiritual person" or "lightworker."

Sense of being specially chosen or gifted.

Pride in spiritual advancement or enlightenment.

And identity based on spiritual experiences or abilities.

Your new biblical identity to embrace:

As a child of God through faith in Jesus Christ.

As a saint called to live in holiness and love by God's Grace.

As a servant equipped to love and serve others.

And a beloved one chosen by God for His purposes.

New identity-building practices begin with studying what Scripture says about your identity in Christ. Practice introducing yourself without spiritual titles or claims. Find value in being God's child rather than spiritual performance. Serve others practically rather than seeking to heal or guide them spiritually.

PROTECTION AND ONGOING FREEDOM

Building Spiritual Discernment

"But solid food is for the mature, for those who have their powers of discernment trained by constant practice." (Hebrews 5:14)

Having been deceived once, you need to learn how to build strong discernment to avoid future deception.

Red Flags to recognize:

Teaching that contradicts clear biblical doctrine.

Practices borrowed from non-Christian religions.

Emphasis on spiritual experiences over biblical truth.

Claims of special revelation beyond Scripture.

Appeals to spiritual pride or superiority.

Discernment-building practices:

Begin with daily prayer—learning how to talk to Papa God in a personal, conversational, non-religious way.

Learning to sense the Spirit of God and **THE PEACE** that passes understanding that rules and guards your heart and mind.

Do regular Bible study; personally and with other trusted good believers.

Possibly some limited study of church history with a view to understanding how deceptions have appeared throughout time.

Understand and learn how to defend biblical truth.

And by developing relationships with biblically mature believers who can help provide guidance.

I highly suggest studying my first two books to learn much more about how to do these things successfully.

Sharing Your Testimony

"They conquered him by the blood of the Lamb and by the word of their testimony." (Revelation 12:11)

Your testimony of freedom can help others trapped in similar deception. You don't need to go out looking for ways to do this, but when the opportunity arises, be ready to share the good things God has done for you.

Important elements to remember:

Honest acknowledgment of your past involvement without defending it.

Clear explanation of how you recognized the deception.

Specific steps you took to find freedom.

The difference between your old spiritual bondage and new freedom in Christ.

And the hope and encouragement for others seeking freedom.

Opportunities to share may happen with friends and family still involved in spiritual deception. In church settings where your story can help others. Online, in forums and groups where people seek truth. Or through writing or speaking about your experience.

HELPING OTHERS FIND FREEDOM

Becoming an Agent of Liberation

Once you've experienced freedom, God may call you to help others escape spiritual deception. You shouldn't seek after this. If it's Papa's will, then opportunities will come without your effort.

How can you prepare yourself?

Be sure your own freedom is solid and stable.

Study Scripture thoroughly to understand biblical truth about spiritual deception.

Learn how to approach people in deception with love rather than condemnation.

Develop relationships with other good believers doing the same.

Only approach them as the Spirit of God leads you in His **Perfect PEACE**. Then you can lead with love and relationship rather than argument. Share your testimony rather than attacking their beliefs. Ask questions that help them examine their own spiritual fruit. Provide practical support during their freedom process. Offer ongoing ways to keep in contact, if they're interested.

Approach with wisdom. Remember not everyone is ready to hear the Truth—always pray for the Holy Spirit's guidance and **THE PEACE**. Remember, many people must experience a crisis before they're open to change. Therefore, you might only be "planting seeds" for the future and must remember to be patient as they are the only ones who can decide for themselves the "if" and/or "when." Trust God's timing rather than trying to force freedom.

SPEAK TO THE DECEIVED

Don't look to create opportunities; but when the time is right, don't be afraid to speak to the deceived. This is a time to enjoy your newfound freedom and share the good news. Yet, as just stated, walk with Papa God and be directed by the Holy Spirit and **HIS PEACE**.

When it's God's timing, don't be afraid to speak to the agnostic. To the atheist. To those in spiritual darkness. Be a light for God for them to see that anything is possible with the One and Only, True and Living God.

Freedom is possible.

You've seen it in this chapter.

Now go live it.

CHAPTER SEVENTEEN

ESCAPING SPIRITUAL DECEPTIONS ~ QUICK REFERENCE GUIDE

FOR EMERGENCY SPIRITUAL DISCERNMENT

Y OU MADE IT THIS far. Good.

Now here's the cheat sheet. The CliffsNotes. The "break glass in case of emergency" chapter.

Because when you're knee-deep in spiritual deception—yours or someone else's—you don't have time to flip through sixteen chapters looking for the right answer.

You need it NOW.

This is that chapter.

"Test everything; hold fast what is good." (1 Thessalonians 5:21)

INSTANT SPIRITUAL PRACTICE EVALUATION

The 5-Minute Test

Don't have time to do a deep theological analysis? Fine. Run anything through these filters. Takes about five minutes. Saves you years of bondage.

IMMEDIATE RED FLAGS

If ANY of these are present, run:

- **Borrowed from non-Christian religions** (yoga, meditation, chakras)

- **Involves spirit contact or guides** ("angels," "ascended masters")

- **Promises power to control circumstances** (manifestation, law of attraction)

- **Requires altered states of consciousness** (emptying mind, breathwork)

- **Claims special revelation beyond Scripture**

- **Uses scientific-sounding language for spiritual claims** (quantum, frequency, vibration)

- **Creates dependency on human practitioners** rather than God

If you see even ONE Red Flag = FULL STOP.

Don't Negotiate.

BIBLICAL GREEN LIGHTS

ALL of these must be present:

- Points to Jesus Christ as the **ONLY** way to God

- Aligns perfectly with Scripture — no exceptions, no "reinterpretations"

- Produces humility and dependence on God

- Brings "**THE PEACE** of God that passes understanding"

- Encourages biblical fellowship and encourages accountability to Papa God

- Promotes love for God and others

- Results in spiritual fruit: love, joy, peace, patience, kindness, goodness, faithfulness, gentleness, self-control

Missing even ONE green light?

Proceed with Extreme Caution.

THE FOUR COMPETING VOICES

This was covered in detail in **SET THE CAPTIVES FREE**, so I'll keep this brief.

Every thought, impression, and "leading" you receive comes from one of four sources:

- God's voice

- Satan's voice

- Your voice

- Other's voices

Which Voice are You Hearing? What Fruit Does it Produce?

YOUR PRIMARY DISCERNMENT TOOL

Does this thing—whatever it is—bring **THE PEACE of God that passes understanding?**

Not, just "a peace." Not, "any peace." Not, "I feel calm."

GOD'S specific PEACE.

You'll know the difference. If you have to convince yourself it's there, it's not.

MODERN DECEPTIONS QUICK REFERENCE

Here's your cheat sheet. What it is, what's wrong with it, what to do instead.

MANIFESTATION & REALITY CONTROL

- **Law of Attraction**—Belief that thoughts create reality
- **Visualization**—Mental techniques to manifest desires
- **Affirmations**—Positive declarations to change circumstances
- **Gratitude Practices**—Using thankfulness to attract outcomes

BIBLICAL ALTERNATIVE:

Prayer with surrender to God's will. You're not in charge. He is.

ENERGY & CONSCIOUSNESS

- **Reiki/Energy Healing**—Channeling "universal life force"
- **Chakras**—Hindu energy centers in the body
- **Crystal Healing**—Using stones for spiritual power

- **Meditation** (emptying the mind)—Altered consciousness practices

BIBLICAL ALTERNATIVE:

Spending time with Jesus, studying Scripture, and prayer. Fill your mind with truth—don't empty it for anything else to fill.

ANCIENT WISDOM

- **Yoga** — Hindu spiritual practice (even "Christian" versions)

- **Eastern Meditation** — Buddhist / Hindu consciousness techniques

- **Shamanism** — Indigenous spirit contact practices

- **Astrology/Tarot** — Divination and fortune-telling

BIBLICAL ALTERNATIVE:

Seek wisdom from God's Word. Period.

HEALING & WELLNESS

- **Sound Healing**—Frequencies for spiritual/physical healing

- **Aromatherapy (spiritual)**—Essential oils with metaphysical claims

- **Past Life Regression**—Healing through supposed previous lives

- **Soul Retrieval**—Shamanic healing for trauma

BIBLICAL ALTERNATIVE:

Biblical counseling and prayer for healing. Jesus is the healer—not frequencies, oils, or past lives.

EMERGENCY SPIRITUAL CRISIS PROTOCOL

Someone's in immediate spiritual danger. What now?

STEP 1: IMMEDIATE PRAYER PROTECTION

CRITICAL: Before you do ANYTHING, you need to have fully studied and learned everything from *THE DAILY STAND* to be able to walk in the Anointing and Stand in God's Authority.

The Prayer:

"Father, in the name of Jesus, we ask for Your protection over [name]. We bind up and cut off any and all evil coming against them. We agree and release You Holy Spirit to surround them. Surround them, as well with Your angels to stand guard over them, their families and all connected. Then give them the clarity to see the darkness and lies they have bought into—and lead them into your Light and Truth. Give them the desire to be set free from this bondage and the humility and Grace to call out to You for themselves for this freedom."

STEP 2: ASSESS THE SITUATION

By the Spirit of God, discern:

- Are they involved in occult practices? (tarot, psychics, spirit guides)

- Experiencing unusual spiritual manifestations?

- Showing signs of spiritual oppression? (fear, confusion, depression)

- Blinded by or under the influence of spiritual teacher(s) or group(s)?

STEP 3: PRAYERFULLY CONSIDER PROVIDING IMMEDIATE HELP

IF CLEARLY BEING LED BY THE SPIRIT OF GOD

If you and those standing with you have **NOT** mastered **THE PEACE** of God and learned to be so directed by the Holy Spirit, then just pray the Prayer Protection (above) and

DO NO MORE.

If you DO have that PEACE, then stay with them—don't leave them alone.

- Pray the Prayer Protection again (above).

- Read Scriptures aloud, such as Psalm 23, John 14, Romans 8 or whatever as the Holy Spirit directs

- You can play Christian worship music if it seems appropriate

- Wait until they calm down

- Ask them if they're ready to give their life and these areas over to the Lord

- If so, then lead them through the Scriptures in how to know Him

CRITICAL:

Remember from the previous "deliverance section," do **NOT** do any "casting out of demons" type of deliverance at this time unless you (and all there) have **THE PERFECT PEACE** of God. Even then, I'd suggest caution as this might not be the correct time for such deliverance. It might just be the time to bring them through this crisis and lead them to the Lord. Let this be the beginning of the "set the captives free" type of deliverance. God will have His perfect timing for all deliverance in all things. So be patient and wait on Him.

AVOID THESE MISTAKES

- **Don't** try to cast out demons without proper training

- **Don't** argue or debate while they're in crisis

- **Don't** leave them to handle it alone until the Spirit of God says to do so

- **Don't** ignore or minimize their experience

FOLLOW-UP CARE

- Connect them with a good local (small) church with good biblical counselor(s) or pastor(s) who you've already vetted as a good church with good leaders as taught in the second book

- Provide ongoing support as the Holy Spirit leads

- Help lead them through the freedom process

- Monitor for continued spiritual attacks

- Continue to pray the Prayer of Protection (above) for them

FREEDOM PROCESS CHECKLIST

For someone wanting to leave spiritual deception.

This isn't a formula. It's a framework. The Holy Spirit leads—you follow.

1. RECOGNITION PHASE

- Acknowledge their involvement in non-biblical practices

- Recognize these practices as spiritually dangerous

- Count the cost of leaving (relationships, money, identity)

- Make a definitive decision to pursue biblical truth

2. CONFESSION PHASE

- Confess involvement in being in rebellion against God

- List specific practices they participated in

- Acknowledge if they lead others into deception

- Always asking God for His forgiveness through Jesus Christ

3. RENUNCIATION PHASE

- Verbally renounce all deceptive practices they participated in any way by name

- Break any and all, known and unknown, spiritual contracts and agreements

- Submit to God in all things and under the blood of Jesus

- Have someone experienced in *THE DAILY STAND* standing with them as they bind up and cut off all connections to all spirits that are behind all these things

- With these same people, loose the Holy Spirit to come backfill all these areas

- Remember, **No** ("casting out of demons" type of) **Deliverance** at this time

- Declare their allegiance to Jesus Christ alone

4. REMOVAL PHASE

- Destroy all books, objects, crystals, cards

- Delete apps, unsubscribe from teachers/channels

- Remove spiritual artwork and symbols

- Cancel memberships in spiritual organizations

5. REPLACEMENT PHASE

- Begin daily Bible reading and prayer

- Find a good biblical church and fellowship

- Replace deceptive practices with biblical ones

- Seek biblical counseling if needed

6. PROTECTION PHASE

- Learn ongoing spiritual discernment

- Build relationships that help keep them accountable to God

- Be ready to share testimony to help others—actually helps them as much as helping others to talk about how God set them free and is continuing to do so

- Start a lifelong process to grow in biblical truth and walk with Papa God

BIBLICAL RESPONSE SCRIPTURES

For specific deceptions:

Manifestation & Law of Attraction

"Many are the plans in the mind of a man, but it is the purpose of the Lord that will stand." (Proverbs 19:21)

Translation: Your thoughts don't create reality. God's will does.

Energy Healing

"And my God will supply every need of yours according to his riches in glory in Christ Jesus." (Philippians 4:19)

Translation: God supplies. Not "universal energy."

Spirit Guides or Angels

"But even if we or an angel from heaven should preach to you a gospel contrary to the one we preached to you, let him be accursed." (Galatians 1:8)

Translation: Not every "angel" is from God.

Divination & Fortune-telling

"There shall not be found among you... anyone who practices divination or tells fortunes." (Deuteronomy 18:10)

Translation: Not "it depends." Not "maybe." SHALL NOT.

Ancient Wisdom

"See to it that no one takes you captive by philosophy and empty deceit, according to human tradition." (Colossians 2:8)

Translation: "Ancient" doesn't mean "true."

Multiple Spiritual Paths

"Jesus said to him, 'I am The Way, and The Truth, and The Life. No one comes to the Father except through me'." (John 14:6)

Translation: One way. Not many. One.

Higher Consciousness

"The fear of the Lord is the beginning of wisdom, and the knowledge of the Holy One is insight" (Proverbs 9:10)

Translation: Wisdom starts with fearing God, not "raising your consciousness."

WARNING SIGNS SOMEONE IS IN SPIRITUAL DECEPTION

People rarely announce they've fallen into deception. Watch for these patterns:

BEHAVIORAL CHANGES

- Increasing isolation from biblical Christians

- Defensive about spiritual practices when questioned

- Using New Age terminology regularly

- Spending significant money on spiritual products or services

- Identity becoming centered on spiritual practices

RELATIONAL CHANGES

- Judging Christians as "less evolved" or "closed-minded"

- Losing close relationships with biblical believers

- Surrounding themselves with like-minded spiritual seekers

- Difficulty maintaining relationships with those who question their practices

SPIRITUAL CHANGES

- Decreased interest in Bible study and church attendance

- Replacing biblical prayer with alternative spiritual practices

- Experiencing unusual spiritual manifestations

- Claiming direct revelation that contradicts Scripture

- Growing pride about spiritual advancement or gifts

MENTAL/EMOTIONAL CHANGES

- Increasing spiritual confusion or instability

- Fear of losing spiritual community or identity

- Mood swings related to spiritual experiences

- Difficulty concentrating on non-spiritual matters

- Obsession with spiritual growth and experiences

COMMON OBJECTIONS & QUICK RESPONSES

"This is just for health/wellness, not spiritual purposes."

Response: Many practices retain their spiritual components regardless of intention. The spiritual roots and effects remain even when presented as purely physical. You don't accidentally stumble into the demonic. You open a door.

"I'm not worshipping other gods; I'm just exploring."

Response: Spiritual exploration outside biblical boundaries opens doors to deceptive influences. God wants to be our ONLY source for all spiritual needs. "Exploring" is just another word for wandering into enemy territory without armor.

"This has really helped me; I feel so much better."

Response: No different than starting on recreational drugs, Satan often provides temporary benefits to hook people into deeper deception. The key is long-term spiritual fruit and biblical alignment. Feeling "better" now doesn't mean you're not being set up for bondage later.

"You're being narrow-minded and judgmental."

Response: Testing spiritual practices against Scripture is biblical wisdom, not judgment. Truth is exclusive by nature, and not all spiritual paths lead to the same place. Jesus was narrow-minded enough to say He was the ONLY way. Take it up with Him.

"Christians have done terrible things too."

Response: Human failures don't invalidate biblical truth. We follow Christ, not imperfect Christians. The issue is whether practices align with Scripture. Christians failing doesn't make yoga safe.

"God gave us these gifts; why wouldn't He want us to use them?"

Response: True spiritual gifts come from God and align with Scripture. Counterfeits come from other sources and contradict biblical truth. The question isn't whether it's a "gift"—the question is who's giving it.

RESOURCES FOR IMMEDIATE HELP

When you may need Expert assistance:

There are good National Organizations, Online Resources, Books, and Podcasts that can help you. You need to ask your local (vetted) people you're working with for the ones they'd recommend with the caveat below.

REMEMBER: If these sources are teaching the correct type of Deliverance—being **Set Free**—with **ALL** foundations and **ALL** cautions laid out in this book, then **PROCEED**. But if they **EVER** discuss, suggest or push "casting out of demons" type of Deliverance to be done sooner versus later, then **STOP IMMEDIATELY** and find another resource.

Find Good Local Help

- Contact a pastor or church leadership of a church [you've vetted from *SET THE CAPTIVES FREE*]

- Search for "biblical counseling" [for your area of concern] in your city

- Ask Christian friends for referrals to experienced counselors [for your area of concern]

- Again: **DO NOT** jump into "Deliverance Ministries" with pastors, leaders, ministers pushing the "casting out of demons"—there may very well be a time for removing the oppression and possession of demons, but it's not **ALWAYS** true and definitely **NOT** in the beginning—the **ONLY Exception** would be if the Holy Spirit is leading and confirming by the **PERFECT PEACE** of God that it is an immediate need; which I don't believe would be the normal

PROTECTION PRAYERS

Please study *THE DAILY STAND* to really understand and take to heart these things for your protection.

DAILY PROTECTION PRAYER

"Lord, help me put on the full armor of God today. I Stand yielded to You. I bind up and cut off all evil that would come against me and my family by the blood of Jesus. I agree with and loose the Holy Spirit and God's angels to stand guard around us. Protect my mind from deceptive thoughts and my heart from spiritual lies. Help me to learn to recognize Your voice and reject all counterfeits. Surround me with Your angels and fill me with Your Spirit. Let **YOUR PERFECT PEACE** rule in and through me. Seal this by Your Spirit."

FOR FAMILY PROTECTION

"Lord, I place my family under Your protection. Guard our home from all spiritual deception. Help us test everything against Your Word and hold fast to what is good. Protect our children from cultural spiritual influences. Seal this by Your Spirit."

FOR SOMEONE IN DECEPTION

"Lord, I pray for [name] who is trapped in spiritual deception. Open their spiritual eyes to see the Truth in You. I stand in agreement with You and all such believers that the power of spiritual blindness and confusion over them will be broken. Send Your Spirit to convince them and draw them to You and Your Truth. Surround them with believers who can help them find freedom. Seal this by Your Spirit."

BEFORE EVER TRYING TO MINISTER TO SOMEONE IN DECEPTION

Number one rule: **DO NOTHING** without clear direction from the Father as well as having **THE PEACE** that passes understanding ruling your heart and mind confirming what you believe you hear Him saying.

But if you do individually or in a group of believers, then:

"Lord, I [we] yield myself [or ourselves] to You and ask for Your protection. I [we] allow You Holy Spirit to flow here in and through this situation. As I [we] Stand yielded to You allowing the Anointing to flow, then and only then can I [we] Stand in Your Authority to see others find freedom. Cover me [us] and this situation by Your blood and surround us by Your angels. Give me [us] **THE PEACE**, Your wisdom, Your love, and Your discernment. Then and only then, see Your power flow to set the captives free and do ONLY what You want done for here and now. "

QUICK DECISION TREE

When Evaluating Any Spiritual Practice

SIX Questions.

SIX Decisions.

NO Wiggle Room.

1. **Does this practice point people to Jesus Christ as the ONLY way to God?** If NO, **AVOID immediately**. If YES, continue evaluation.

2. **Does this practice align with clear biblical teaching?** If

NO, **AVOID regardless of claimed benefits**. If UNCLEAR, research thoroughly before participating. If YES, continue evaluation.

3. **Does this practice require techniques borrowed from other religions?** If YES, **AVOID all spiritual fusion of belief systems as dangerous**. If NO, continue evaluation.

4. **Does this practice produce "THE PEACE of God that passes understanding?"** If NO, **AVOID—lack of God's PEACE is a warning sign**. If YES, continue evaluation.

5. **Does this practice promote humility and dependence on God?** If NO, **AVOID—spiritual pride is a danger sign**. If YES, continue with discernment and remaining accountable before God.

6. **Does this practice produce biblical spiritual fruit in your life?** If NO, **STOP and reevaluate**. If YES, continue moving forward; but always MONITORING it with ongoing discernment by the Holy Spirit.

FINAL REMINDERS

CORE TRUTHS TO REMEMBER

- **Jesus Christ is the ONLY way to the Father**—John 14:6

- **Scripture is our final authority** for all spiritual matters—2 Timothy 3:16

- **We only see, hear, and know in part**—maintain humility—1 Corinthians 13:12

- **THE PEACE of God** is our primary discernment tool —Philippians 4:7

- **Freedom is possible** for anyone trapped in spiritual deception—John 8:32

REMEMBER PAPA'S HEART

- You are dealing with **captives, not enemies**

- Approach with **God's Love**, not condemnation

- Trust **God's Power** to set people free

- **You are not alone** in this spiritual battle.

- **Victory is certain** through Christ Jesus

WHEN IN DOUBT

- **Pray first** before acting

- **Consult Scripture** for guidance

- **Seek wise counsel** from mature believers

- **Trust God's timing** rather than forcing outcomes

- **Remember:** It's better to be cautious than compromised

THE BOTTOM LINE

If you're trapped in spiritual deception:

Freedom is possible through Jesus Christ. Start with honest confession, complete renunciation, and total surrender to God's Truth. Not partial. Not "most of it." **TOTAL**.

If you're helping someone else:

Approach with Papa's heart of Love. Be patient, provide biblical truth, and trust God's timing for their freedom. You can't force liberation. You can only point the way and walk alongside.

If you're protecting yourself/family:

Build strong biblical foundations, maintain spiritual discernment, and stay connected to a biblical community. The best defense is a deep offense—know the Word and **THE PEACE** so well that counterfeits stand out immediately.

Remember: The same power that raised Jesus from the dead is available to set every captive free and protect every believer who stands firm in biblical truth.

That power isn't in techniques. It isn't in rituals. It isn't in "energy."

It's in a Person. And His name is Jesus.

~~~~~

"The Spirit of the Lord is upon me...

to SET the OPPRESSED [CAPTIVES] FREE."

(Luke 4:18)

CHAPTER EIGHTEEN

FREEDOM FROM...

YOUR CONSOLIDATED ACTION GUIDE

Y OU'VE READ THE CHAPTERS. You've seen the deceptions exposed. You've probably recognized yourself—or someone you love—in more than one of them.

Now what?

This chapter isn't about explaining why these things are dangerous. We've done that. This chapter is about how to get free. Action steps. Specific prayers. Concrete renunciations.

Consider this your consolidated extraction plan.

Because knowing you're trapped and actually getting out are two very different things.

"But Tom, I already read the other chapters!"

Great. Then you know why you need to act. This is the HOW.

Pick your deception. Follow the steps. Get free.

FREEDOM FROM MANIFESTATION PRACTICES

Includes: Law of Attraction, visualization, affirmations, vision boards, "speaking things into existence," prosperity gospel techniques

THE LIE YOU BELIEVED

Your thoughts create reality. You can manipulate spiritual forces to get what you want. You're a "co-creator" with the universe.

Translation: You wanted to be God rather than submit to God.

THE FREEDOM STEPS

1. **Confess** the desire to be a god rather than submit to God. Recognize manifestation as a form of witchcraft and spiritual manipulation.

2. **Repent** to God; ask Him into your life (He promises He will come in and seal you with His Holy Spirit); and give Him the permission to be in charge of your life.

3. **Renounce** all involvement in manifestation techniques and teachings. Be specific: "I renounce the Law of Attraction. I

renounce visualization for manifesting. I renounce speaking things into existence apart from God's will. Etc..."

4. **Destroy** books, materials, and objects related to these practices. Vision boards. Manifestation journals. All of it.

5. **Break** any spiritual agreements or declarations made during manifestation practices. Have someone experienced in *THE DAILY STAND* stand with you as you bind up and cut off all connections to all spirits behind all these things.

6. **Ask** God for His forgiveness for seeking to manipulate spiritual forces.

THE REPLACEMENT

Learn biblical prayer as communion with God rather than spiritual manipulation. Practice surrender and trust instead of trying to control outcomes. Find identity in being God's child rather than a spiritual creator. And develop contentment and gratitude based on God's goodness rather than circumstances.

Then you will be able to learn biblical prayer as communion with God, rather than spiritual manipulation.

FREEDOM FROM ANCIENT WISDOM DECEPTIONS

Includes: Eastern mysticism, yoga, shamanism, indigenous spirituality, Kabbalah, Gnosticism, Western occultism

THE LIE YOU BELIEVED

That "ancient" means "true." That other cultures discovered spiritual secrets the Bible missed. That you could cherry-pick the "good parts" without spiritual consequences.

Translation: You thought recycled paganism looked better in exotic packaging.

THE FREEDOM STEPS

1. **Recognize** and acknowledge that "ancient wisdom" often represents recycled paganism. Recognize that spiritual practices have spiritual consequences regardless of cultural packaging. Understand that God's wisdom revealed in Scripture is superior to human wisdom.

2. **Accept** that those practices, condemned in Scripture, remain dangerous today.

3. **Renounce** all involvement with Eastern mysticism, shamanism, and Western occultism. Be specific about each practice: yoga, meditation techniques, spirit guides, power animals, etc.

4. **Destroy** all books, objects, and materials related to these practices.

5. **Break** any spiritual commitments or initiations made in these traditions. Have someone experienced in *THE DAILY STAND* stand with you.

6. **Ask** God's forgiveness for seeking wisdom from sources other than Him.

THE REPLACEMENT

Ground all spiritual seeking in biblical study and prayer. Find fellowship with believers committed to biblical authority. Develop discernment to recognize occult practices regardless of packaging. Learn from church history to understand how these deceptions have appeared throughout time.

FREEDOM FROM ENERGY & CONSCIOUSNESS PRACTICES

Includes: Reiki, chakras, crystal healing, energy work, aura reading, quantum mysticism, consciousness expansion

THE LIE YOU BELIEVED

There's a "universal life force" you can tap into. Your body has "energy centers" that need balancing. Rocks have healing power. That "higher consciousness" is the goal.

Translation: You fell for Hinduism wrapped in pseudoscientific language.

THE FREEDOM STEPS

1. **Recognize** that "energy" practices are spiritual, not scientific. The "universal life force" isn't neutral—it's an alternative to the Holy Spirit.

2. **Renounce** all energy healing practices by name: Reiki, chakra work, crystal healing, energy balancing, etc.

3. **Renounce** any attunements, initiations, or "openings" received.

4. **Destroy** crystals used for spiritual purposes, Reiki materials, chakra charts, etc.

5. **Break** connection to any "spirit guides" or "healing masters" encountered during these practices. Have someone experienced in *THE DAILY STAND* stand with you as you bind up and cut off.

6. **Ask** God to fill you with His Holy Spirit—the only "energy" you need.

THE REPLACEMENT

For healing: pray, seek medical care (as needed), and trust God's sovereignty.

For PEACE: learn to meditate on Scripture and get God's True PEACE [as learned in Philippians 4:7].

For spiritual power: seek the Holy Spirit's filling through yielding to God [as learned in John 7:38-39].

FREEDOM FROM DIVINATION & FORTUNE-TELLING

Includes: Tarot, astrology, palm reading, psychics, mediums, Ouija boards, horoscopes, numerology

THE LIE YOU BELIEVED

You could know the future through forbidden means. The stars control your destiny. Dead people can be contacted. That it's "just for fun."

Translation: You wanted insider information without going through God.

THE FREEDOM STEPS

1. **Recognize** that all divination is explicitly forbidden in Scripture (Deuteronomy 18:10-12). NO exceptions. Not even "for entertainment."

2. **Renounce** all divination practices by name: "I renounce tarot cards. I renounce astrology. I renounce consulting psychics. Etc..."

3. **Destroy** tarot decks, astrology books, Ouija boards, crystals used for divination—ALL of it.

4. **Renounce** any "spirit guides" or entities contacted during divination. Have someone experienced in *THE DAILY STAND* stand with you.

5. **Repent** for seeking knowledge outside of God's revealed will.

THE REPLACEMENT

For guidance: pray, study Scripture, seek godly counsel.

For the future: trust God's sovereignty. Accept that some things aren't for you to know—and that's okay.

FREEDOM FROM SPIRITUAL HEALING

COUNTERFEITS

Includes: Sound healing, past life regression, soul retrieval, spiritual aromatherapy, faith healers (false ones), (non-Biblical) inner healing

THE LIE YOU BELIEVED

Frequencies heal. Your problems come from "past lives." Someone can retrieve pieces of your soul. That essential oils have spiritual power.

Translation: You wanted healing without the Healer.

THE FREEDOM STEPS

1. **Recognize** that Jesus is the healer—not frequencies, not past lives, not "soul retrieval."

2. **Renounce** all counterfeit healing practices: "I renounce past life regression. I renounce soul retrieval. I renounce sound healing for spiritual purposes. Etc..."

3. **Reject** the concept of reincarnation—you have one life (Hebrews 9:27).

4. **Cancel** any "healing" received from false sources. Have someone experienced in *THE DAILY STAND* stand with you.

5. **Ask** God for true healing — physical, emotional, and spiritual — through Jesus Christ.

THE REPLACEMENT

Seek biblical counseling for emotional wounds.

Pray for healing while also pursuing appropriate medical care.

Trust God's timing and sovereignty over your health.

Remember: sometimes healing comes in eternity, not on earth.

FREEDOM FROM "CHRISTIAN" COUNTERFEITS

Includes: False prophets, false NAR practices, contemplative prayer, "soaking," grave sucking, kundalini in church, false signs and wonders

THE LIE YOU BELIEVED

That because it happened in church, it must be from God. That supernatural experiences validate teaching. That questioning leaders is wrong and means lacking faith.

Translation: You trusted the packaging more than the product.

THE FREEDOM STEPS

1. **Test everything against Scripture**—even (especially) what happens in church. Signs and wonders don't validate truth.

2. **Renounce the false teachings you accepted**: "I renounce the false prophecies I received. I renounce contemplative prayer. I renounce practices borrowed from Eastern religions and repackaged as Christian."

3. **Break "soul ties" and any ties with false teachers and movements.** Have someone experienced in *THE DAILY*

301

STAND stand with you.

4. **Repent** for elevating experience over Scripture.

5. **Find** a biblically grounded [vetted] church with leaders committed to Scripture's authority.

THE REPLACEMENT

Ground all spiritual practice in Scripture.

Value sound teaching over emotional experiences.

Choose fellowship that encourages biblical testing.

Remember: the most dangerous counterfeits look the most like the real thing.

FREEDOM FROM SELF-WORSHIP PRACTICES

Includes: "Higher self," self-actualization, "you are enough," human potential movement, self-as-god thinking

THE LIE YOU BELIEVED

You are divine. All the answers are within you. You're "enough" without God. That self-improvement is salvation.

Translation: You bought the original lie from Eden: "You will be like God."

THE FREEDOM STEPS

1. **Confess** the pride of self-worship. You're not divine. You're not enough on your own. You need a Savior.

2. **Renounce** "higher self" thinking, self-actualization as a spiritual goal, and human potential spirituality.

3. **Accept** your identity as God's creation, fallen but redeemable through Christ alone.

4. **Embrace** dependence on God rather than self-sufficiency.

5. **Find** identity in being God's child rather than in personal achievement or spiritual advancement.

THE REPLACEMENT

True self-worth comes from being created and loved by God—not from being divine yourself.

Growth comes through dying to self, not elevating self.

Fulfillment comes through serving God and others, not self-actualization.

THE COMMON THREAD

Notice anything?

Every single deception offers the same thing: **power apart from submission to God.**

Manifestation: power to control reality.

Ancient wisdom: power through secret knowledge.

Energy practices: power over spiritual forces.

Divination: power to know the future.

Counterfeit healing: power over health and wholeness.

False Christianity: power through supernatural experiences.

Self-worship: power through self-divinity.

Same lie. Different packaging.

"You will be like God" (Genesis 3:5).

The enemy has exactly one playbook.

He just keeps changing the cover.

THE FREEDOM PATTERN

Regardless of which deception trapped you, freedom follows the same pattern:

- **RECOGNIZE** the deception for what it is

- **REPENT** to God for participating

- **RENOUNCE** specific practices by name

- **REMOVE** all related materials

- **BREAK** spiritual agreements and connections

- **REPLACE** with biblical truth and practice

- **REMAIN** accountable to God along with mature believers

Simple? YES.

Easy? NO.

But Possible. Through Jesus Christ, Absolutely Possible.

THE BOTTOM LINE

You might have been involved in one of these areas. You might have been involved in several. You might be looking at this list thinking, "That's practically my whole spiritual history."

Doesn't matter.

The blood of Jesus covers it all. Every deception. Every practice. Every agreement. Every lie you believed.

ALL of it.

But YOU have to CHOOSE freedom.

YOU have to actively renounce what you actively embraced.

YOU can't just passively drift into liberty—you have to march out of Egypt.

And when YOU do—when you confess, repent, renounce, and receive God's forgiveness—

YOU'RE FREE.

Not "kind of" free. Not "working toward" free.

FREE.

**"So if the Son sets you FREE, you will be FREE indeed."
— John 8:36**

~~~

"Stand fast therefore in the liberty by which Christ has made us FREE, and do not be entangled again with a yoke of bondage." — Galatians 5:1

CHAPTER NINETEEN

WHAT IF WOO IS A MASQUERADE?

WHEN THE PARTY'S OVER AND THE MASK COMES OFF

W HAT IF THE DECEPTIONS led you straight into the arms of the enemy?

What if, at the end of all your searching, you found something that wanted to destroy you?

And what if you're living in that destruction right now?

Then, this chapter is for you.

Not the curious reader. Not the person who dabbled a little and walked away. Not the one who's mildly concerned about a friend.

This chapter is for the one who's drowning.

THE REALITY CHECK

Maybe you picked up this book because you've fallen into a deep depression and you can't find the bottom.

Maybe you feel utterly without hope—like the lights went out and nobody's coming to turn them back on.

Maybe you feel oppressed. Or possessed. Like something got inside you that you can't get out.

Maybe you've become suicidal.

I need you to hear something:

That's not an accident. That's the plan.

THE MASQUERADE REVEALED

See, the "Woo" never told you where it was really leading, did it?

The manifestation coaches didn't mention the depression that would follow when the universe "didn't deliver."

The energy healers didn't warn you about the spiritual attachments that would come with those "attunements."

The psychics didn't tell you that opening those doors would invite things through that don't leave when the session ends.

The yoga instructor didn't explain that those "kundalini awakenings" sometimes look a lot like demonic manifestations.

"But it felt so good at first!"

Of course it did.

The bait always tastes good. That's why it's bait.

WHAT YOU'RE ACTUALLY DEALING WITH

Let me be blunt with you, because I think you can handle it. Actually, I think you need someone to be blunt with you.

The "Woo" was never just Woo.

It was a Masquerade.

Behind the pretty masks of "enlightenment" and "awakening" and "higher consciousness" and "manifesting your best life"—

There are faces.

Just NOT Human Faces.

Faces that have been wearing masks since Eden.

"You will be like God."

Same lie. Same liar. Same destination.

And that destination was never enlightenment. It was enslavement.

THE SYMPTOMS NOBODY WARNED YOU ABOUT

If you've gone deep into Woo, you might be experiencing things like:

- **Depression that came out of nowhere** and won't respond to normal treatment

- **Suicidal thoughts** that feel like they're not even yours—like they're being pushed into your mind

- **A sense of presence** in your home or around you that feels heavy, dark, or threatening

- **Sleep disturbances:** nightmares, sleep paralysis, waking at the same time every night—often in the middle of the night

- **Physical symptoms** doctors can't explain

- **Hearing voices** or intrusive thoughts that mock, accuse, or torment you

- **Inability to read the Bible, pray, or go to church** without intense resistance or physical reaction

- **Feeling cut off from** God, like there's a wall between you and Him that you can't break through

- **Rage, fear, or despair** that comes in waves and doesn't match your circumstances

Sound familiar?

That's not mental illness.

That's not "bad energy."

That's not your chakras being out of alignment.

That's spiritual bondage. And it has a solution.

"BUT I WAS JUST TRYING TO FIND MYSELF"

I know.

I know you weren't trying to open doors to darkness. I know you thought you were on a journey of self-discovery. I know you believed the people who told you this would bring peace, healing, enlightenment.

They Lied to You.

Or they were deceived themselves and passed the deception along.

Either way, here you are.

And here's the good news:

The one who has the power to free you,

actually wants to.

THE WAY OUT

Jesus Christ didn't come to give you a better meditation technique.

He didn't come to raise your vibration.

He didn't come to help you manifest your dreams.

He came to Set Captives Free.

"The Spirit of the Lord is upon Me, because He has anointed Me to preach the gospel to the poor; He has sent Me to **heal the brokenhearted**, to **proclaim liberty to the captives** and **recovery of sight to the blind**, to **set at liberty those who are oppressed**." — Luke 4:18

That's you. The captive. The oppressed. The one who went looking for light and found darkness instead.

He came for YOU.

IF YOU'RE HAVING SUICIDAL THOUGHTS

Stop right here.

I need you to understand something critical:

Those thoughts are not yours.

They're being pushed into your mind by something that wants you dead. Something that knows your death would:

1. **Cut off** your Chance to be free

2. **Stop** you from Finding the true freedom God has waiting for you

3. **Rob** you from Finding what God has planned for the rest of your life

4. **Hurt** everyone who loves you

5. **Prevent** you from warning others

Don't let him win.

Right now, out loud, say this:

"Because of the blood of Jesus Christ, that I receive right now, I reject every suicidal thought. I command every spirit of death and suicide to be quiet, now, and stay quiet. I choose life. I choose to fight. I choose to get free. Holy Spirit of God please help me to do all these things."

Now call someone. A pastor. A Christian friend. A crisis line. Don't stay alone with this.

YOUR story isn't over.

YOUR end hasn't been written yet.

STAY alive to find out what's ahead.

CHOOSE to live to tell it.

IMMEDIATE STEPS FOR THE DESPERATE

If you're in crisis right now, here's what you do:

STEP 1: CRY OUT TO JESUS

NOT to the universe. NOT to your higher self. NOT to any spirit guide or ascended master.

To Jesus ALONE.

"Jesus, I need You. I'm in over my head. I opened doors I shouldn't have opened. I'm trapped and I can't get out on my own. Please help me. Please save me. Please set me free."

That's it. That's enough to start. Continue to pray this each day and as often as you feel it's needed.

STEP 2: RENOUNCE OUT LOUD

Name the specific practices you were involved in and renounce them verbally:

"By the blood of Jesus, I renounce [manifestation / Reiki / tarot / yoga / psychics / etc]. I renounce every spirit I contacted through these practices. I renounce every agreement I made, knowingly or unknowingly. I break every tie, every bond, every attachment. I belong to Jesus Christ and no other."

Continue to pray this each day and as often as you feel it's needed.

STEP 3: COMMAND THEM TO STOP AND BE STILL

If *you've received Jesus* as your Lord and Savior and *you're yielding to Him*, you have His authority flowing through you by the Spirit of God:

"By the blood of Jesus, I command every unclean spirit that entered through my involvement with [practices] to stop and be quiet now. You have no legal right to me. I belong to Jesus Christ. Be still now. I choose to never give you permission in my life ever again."

Continue to pray this each day and as often as you feel it's needed.

STEP 4: GET HELP

You shouldn't walk this road alone. Find:

- **A [vetted, good] pastor** who believes in being delivered from Woo—"the healthy way"

- **A mature Christian** who can pray with you and Stand with you

- **Someone** trained in ***THE DAILY STAND***

Freedom often requires backup. There's no shame in that—it's how the body of Christ is supposed to work.

WHAT COMES AFTER

Getting free isn't a onetime event. It's a battle won, but there will be more battles. Prepare yourself with ***THE DAILY STAND*** to learn how to walk with the Spirit of God daily, minute-by-minute, moment-by-moment.

The enemy doesn't give up easily. He'll test your freedom. He'll try to get you back.

Here's how you stay free:

- **STAY in the Word.** The Bible isn't just good advice—it's your sword. Read it daily. Memorize it. Speak it out loud when the attacks come.

- **STAY in prayer.** Not chanting. Not meditation. Actual conversation with your Heavenly Father, who loves you and has your back.

- **STAY in community.** The enemy picks off isolated sheep. Get connected to a solid, vetted, Bible-believing church.

- **STAY accountable.** To God and with solid believers. Tell someone your story. Let them check in on you. Don't carry this alone.

- **STAY alert.** "Be sober, be vigilant; because your adversary the devil walks about like a roaring lion, seeking whom he may devour" (1 Peter 5:8).

- **NEVER go back.** Not "just to see." Not "just for old time's sake." Not "just because it's what my friends are into." The door MUST stay closed. Period.

THE TESTIMONY WAITING TO BE WRITTEN

Here's what I know about you:

You're not reading this by accident.

Somebody prayed for you. Maybe a parent. Maybe a grandparent. Maybe someone you don't even know yet.

And God answered that prayer by putting this book in your hands at exactly this moment.

You were supposed to find this chapter.

Because you have a testimony waiting to be written.

Not a testimony of destruction.

A testimony of being set free from captivity and bondage.

A testimony that will set other people free.

The very depth of your bondage will become the height of your testimony. The darker the pit you came out of, the brighter the light of what God did for you.

That's worth living for.

That's worth fighting for.

THE BOTTOM LINE

Woo was a Masquerade.

The masks are off now. You've seen what's really behind them.

And yeah, it's terrifying.

But here's what's more terrifying to the enemy:

You found out.

You're fighting back.

You're calling on the ONE Name that makes demons tremble.

And He answers.

"Then they cried out to the Lord in their trouble, and He delivered them out of their distresses." — Psalm 107:6

Cry out.

He hears you.

And He will deliver.

~~~

"And they overcame him by the blood of the Lamb and by the word of their testimony." — Revelation 12:11

CHAPTER TWENTY

HELPING OTHERS FIND FREEDOM

APPROACHING CAPTIVES WITH PAPA'S HEART

MINISTERING TO THE DECEIVED

S O YOU WANT TO help someone trapped in spiritual deception.

Noble. Really.

But before you charge in like a spiritual SWAT team ready to rescue the hostages, let me ask you something:

Do you actually love them? Or do you just want to be

seen as right?

Because there's a massive difference. And the deceived person can SMELL the difference a mile away.

Nothing turns someone off to the truth faster than a self-righteous Bible-thumper who's more interested in winning an argument than winning a soul. "Let me show you all the ways you're wrong!" Yeah, that approach is really working out for the church. That's why everyone's flocking to Christianity, right?

Oh wait.

Here's the deal: These are God's children who've been trapped by the enemy's lies. They need liberation, not condemnation. Your role is to be an agent of Papa's Love and Truth—helping set captives free just like Jesus came to do.

Remember what Jesus saw when He looked at the crowds?

"**He had compassion for them**, because they were **harassed** and **helpless**, like sheep without a shepherd." (Matthew 9:36)

Compassion. Not condemnation. Not "I told you so." Not spiritual superiority.

Compassion.

THEY'RE VICTIMS, NOT VILLAINS

Most people trapped in spiritual deception aren't evil. They're not stupid.

They're sincere seekers who:

- Had a genuine hunger for spiritual reality

- Often experienced disappointment or hurt in traditional Christianity

- Were seeking healing, purpose, or spiritual power

- Fell for deceptions that appeared beneficial and enlightening

- Are now trapped in bondage they don't recognize

Sound familiar? It should. That describes EVERY one of us.

The Nature of Their Bondage

Spiritual Blindness: "The god of this world has **blinded the minds** of the unbelievers." (2 Corinthians 4:4)

They literally cannot see the deception. Their spiritual vision has been clouded by demonic influence. What seems obviously false to you seems true to them.

They need a spiritual eye-opening, not more arguments.

Mental Programming: Their thinking has been systematically programmed with lies. They've developed entire worldviews based on deceptive foundations. Questioning these beliefs feels like questioning their identity.

Changing their minds requires more than intellectual arguments. It requires the Spirit of God.

Emotional Investment: They've invested time, money, and relationships in their beliefs. Their identity and social connections are tied to these practices. Leaving would mean losing community, purpose, and spiritual experiences.

Fear of loss keeps them bound even when they sense problems.

Spiritual Oppression: Actual demonic entities work to keep them in bondage. They may experience spiritual attacks when they consider leaving. Confusion and fear increase when they're exposed to biblical truth.

They need spiritual warfare support, not just counseling.

"But Tom, if they just read their Bible, they could figure it out!"

Maybe they could. Maybe not. Should we just "hope for the best" seeing that they weren't on the right path before? Should we just "hope" they can NOW figure out how to navigate the spiritual realm?

Remember your own journey to get here. Like you've never been deceived about anything? Like you've never believed something wrong? Like you figured out everything on your own without anyone helping you?

Get over yourself.

JESUS' MODEL FOR SETTING CAPTIVES FREE

He Approached with Compassion—not condemnation. He recognized they were victims of spiritual predators. His motivation was love and a desire to help—not to prove He was right. He offered hope and healing rather than judgment.

He Spoke Truth in Love—Jesus never compromised Truth to make people comfortable. But He spoke Truth in ways that revealed God's love and desire for relationship. He met people where they were while leading them to where they needed to be.

He Demonstrated God's Power—Jesus backed up His words with demonstrations of God's genuine power. He showed that God's power was superior to all demonic counterfeits. His life proved that biblical Truth produces better fruit than deception.

Paul's Approach

"For as I walked around and looked carefully at your objects of worship, I even found an altar with this inscription: TO AN UNKNOWN GOD. So you are ignorant of the very thing you worship—and this is what I am going to proclaim to you." (Acts 17:23)

Paul took the time to understand what people believed and why. He found points of connection before introducing biblical Truth. He demonstrated respect for people while rejecting their false beliefs. He spoke their language while introducing God's Truth.

And he didn't just tear down false beliefs—he replaced them with biblical Truth. He showed how the gospel met the same needs that false beliefs promised to meet.

FIVE STRATEGIES THAT ACTUALLY WORK

Strategy 1: Most Important is Prayer

Preparation

Pray for spiritual protection over yourself and your family. Ask God to prepare the hearts of those you'll be talking to. Pray for wisdom, love, and discernment in your approach. And bind and cut off all demonic forces that would resist liberation efforts.

Strategy 2: Build Relationship Next

Show genuine interest in them as people and what they care about, not just conversion projects. Spend time together in non-confrontational settings. Demonstrate Christ's love through practical service and care. Be patient with their process rather than demanding immediate change. You can do all this without entering into their Woo.

Learn how they got involved in spiritual deception. Identify the hunger that drove them there. Show empathy in their spiritual seeking rather than judgment.

Let them see the fruit of biblical Christianity in your life. Show them that Christians can be spiritually vibrant AND intellectually honest.

Strategy 3: Ask Strategic Questions

Rather than attacking their beliefs directly, ask questions that help them examine their own spiritual fruit:

Questions About Fruit: "How has this spiritual path affected your relationships?" "Do you feel more peaceful and joyful since you started?" "Have these beliefs helped you become more loving and humble?"

Questions About Authority: "How do you determine which spiritual teachers to trust?" "What standard do you use to evaluate spiritual truth claims?" "How do you know when a spiritual experience is genuine or counterfeit?"

Questions About Consistency: "How do you reconcile contradictions between different spiritual teachers?" "What happens when your spiritual experiences don't match your beliefs?" "Do you ever feel pressure to defend beliefs that don't fully make sense?"

Strategy 4: Share Your Story

Your story of transformation carries more weight than arguments. People can argue with theology but can't argue with changed lives.

Be honest about your mistakes without defending past involvement. Focus on God's Grace and Mercy rather than your spiritual achievement. Acknowledge the difficulty of change while emphasizing the benefits. Offer hope that freedom is possible for them too.

Strategy 5: Provide Biblical Alternatives

People in spiritual deception are usually trying to meet legitimate needs through illegitimate means. Use the resources in this book to understand the teachings and practices they're involved in so you're prepared to answer. Prepare biblical responses to their likely objections and questions. Show them how biblical Christianity meets these same needs more effectively:

- Instead of energy healing → prayer for the sick in Jesus' name

- Instead of visualization and manifestation → biblical prayer and trust in God's provision

- Instead of meditation on emptiness → meditation on Scripture

- Instead of spirit guides → relationship with the Holy Spirit

- Instead of spiritual groups → biblical church fellowship

- Instead of karma and reincarnation → the biblical hope of resurrection and eternal life

WHEN IT GETS HARD

The Challenge: Spiritual Pride

Deceived people often feel spiritually superior to "traditional" Christians. They may view biblical believers as less evolved or enlightened.

Response: Demonstrate intellectual depth and spiritual vitality in biblical Christianity. Help them understand that humility, not pride, marks true spiritual maturity.

The Challenge: Fear of Loss

Fear of losing spiritual community, identity, and invested time keeps people bound.

Response: Acknowledge that the losses are real and the fears are legitimate. Share your own story of loss and how God replaced what was lost with something better. Provide practical support during the transition.

The Challenge: Demonic Resistance

Spiritual attacks may increase when people consider leaving deception. Confusion and fear intensify when they're exposed to biblical truth.

Response: Recognize this as spiritual warfare requiring prayer and spiritual authority. Don't try to handle serious demonic issues without experienced help. Provide ongoing prayer support and spiritual covering.

The Challenge: Intellectual Objections

They've been taught that biblical Christianity is intellectually inferior. They may use scientific-sounding language to defend their beliefs.

Response: Study *THE DAILY STAND* and *SET THE CAPTIVES FREE* so you can be sure you understand and have implemented those answers for yourself before trying to help them. Find other [vetted] Christian believers who can address their specific objections. Help them understand that true science and biblical truth are not in conflict.

THE BOTTOM LINE

Liberation is ultimately about demonstrating Papa God's heart for His deceived children.

- **Love over Judgment:** Approaching people with compassion rather than condemnation

- **Patience over Pressure:** Allowing God's timing rather than forcing immediate change

- **Relationship over Argument:** Building trust and friendship rather than winning debates

- **Truth over Compromise:** Maintaining biblical truth while expressing it in love

- **Hope over Condemnation:** Offering real hope for freedom and transformation

Remember: You're partnering with Papa God by the Holy Spirit in His work of setting captives free. Trust His heart, follow His methods, and depend on His Power to bring His children home to Truth and Freedom.

Because that's what Papa does.

He Sets the Captives Free.

CHAPTER TWENTY-ONE

PROTECTING THE CHURCH FROM DECEPTION

BUILDING SPIRITUAL IMMUNITY IN THE BODY OF CHRIST

The Church's Vulnerability

THE MODERN CHURCH FACES an unprecedented challenge.

Spiritual deceptions are more sophisticated, appealing, and widespread than ever before. And they don't announce themselves as such—they come disguised as beneficial, enlightening, and even "Christian" practices that

329

promise to enhance spiritual life while actually leading believers away from biblical truth.

Protecting the church from deception requires more than defensive measures—it requires building spiritual immunity through biblical knowledge, discernment training, and a strong biblical community that can recognize and resist spiritual threats before they take root.

They're in your bookstore.

In your wellness center.

In your therapy sessions.

And yes—in your churches.

"Not MY church!"

Really?

Have you checked what's being taught in the small groups? Reviewed the books in your church library? Investigated the "Christian" conferences your members attend? Examined the "spiritual formation" practices being promoted?

You need to.

Let me tell you—the infiltration is deeper than most pastors, leaders and believers want to admit.

THE PERFECT STORM FOR

DECEPTION

Cultural Factors

- Postmodern rejection of Absolute Truth creates openness to multiple spiritual paths

- New Age concepts normalized through media, education, and healthcare

- Eastern mysticism is packaged as wellness and self-improvement

- Occult practices presented as entertainment and personal empowerment

Church Factors

- Shallow biblical teaching leaves believers vulnerable to error

- Emphasis on experience over doctrine creates susceptibility to spiritual counterfeits

- The desire for church growth leads to compromise with cultural trends

- Lack of discernment training leaves believers unable to recognize deception

Individual Factors

- Biblical illiteracy prevents recognition of contradictory teachings

- Spiritual hunger seeks satisfaction through any available means

- Disappointment with traditional Christianity creates openness to alternatives

- Lack of an authentic Christian community leaves people seeking belonging elsewhere

"But we're just trying to be relevant!"

Sure.

Because what the church really needs is to be more like the world. That's been working out so well. People are definitely coming to Christ in droves because churches have yoga classes and teach the Enneagram.

Oh wait. They're not. They're leaving. In record numbers.

Maybe—just maybe—the answer isn't to become more like the deception. Maybe it's to become more distinct from it.

HOW DECEPTION ENTERS THE CHURCH

Through Well-Meaning Leaders

Pastors who adopt secular psychology mixed with spiritual techniques. Worship leaders who incorporate Eastern meditation practices. Children's ministers who use "harmless" occult-themed materials. Christian educators who promote "Christian" yoga and mindfulness.

Most of them don't know what they're doing. They've

been deceived themselves.

Through Popular Christian Authors

Books that mix biblical concepts with New Age teachings. "Christian" self-help that promotes manifestation techniques. Spiritual formation books that incorporate Eastern mysticism. Bible studies that use non-biblical spiritual practices.

Just because it's in a Christian bookstore doesn't make it Christian.

Through Christian Conferences and Retreats

Speakers who promote contemplative spirituality. Workshops teaching "Christian" energy healing. Prayer methods borrowed from Eastern religions. Spiritual formation practices that empty rather than fill the mind with Scripture.

Through Christian Counseling and Healing

Therapists who mix biblical counseling with New Age techniques. Healing ministries that incorporate energy work and chakra concepts. Deliverance ministries that adopt shamanic practices. Biblical counseling that includes visualization and guided imagery.

BUILDING SPIRITUAL

IMMUNITY

Just as physical immunity protects against disease, spiritual immunity protects against deception.

Strong Biblical Teaching

- Pure study of the Word / Bible / Scriptures—not limited by any one translation—always including the original texts in the Greek and Hebrew

- Regular expository preaching and teaching that walk through the entire books of Scripture

- Bible study methods that teach people to interpret Scripture correctly

- Spending a limited time exposing church history to show how deceptions have appeared throughout time

Doctrinal Clarity

- Defining true doctrine according to the Word versus church belief systems—see *SET THE CAPTIVES FREE* for clarity

- Debunking and removing false Belief Systems—again see *SET THE CAPTIVES FREE*

- Clear statements of faith according to the Word that address contemporary spiritual issues

- Regular teaching on the nature of God, salvation, and spiritual warfare—see *THE DAILY STAND* on how to do these things

- Explicit rejection of practices that contradict biblical truth

- Ongoing education about the exclusivity of Christ and biblical authority

Discernment Training

- Teaching believers how to test spiritual claims against Scripture

- Training in recognizing the tactics and strategies of spiritual deception

- Practical exercises in distinguishing biblical truth from counterfeit spirituality

- Regular examination of contemporary spiritual trends in light of Scripture

CREATING A CULTURE OF BIBLICAL TRUTH

Leadership Commitment

- Church leaders must be committed to biblical authority over cultural accommodation

- Regular leadership training in discernment and spiritual warfare

- Clear oversight that prevents compromise through deceptive practices

- Clear policies regarding acceptable spiritual practices and teaching methods

Congregation Education

- Regular teaching series on spiritual warfare, spiritual deception and discernment—using *THE DAILY STAND* and *SET THE CAPTIVES FREE*

- Small group studies that address contemporary spiritual challenges

- Studies of biblical worldview and how to help those in spiritual need

- Youth and children's programs that build strong biblical foundations

Community holding each other Accountable to God

- Church oversight that addresses involvement in deceptive practices

- Encouragement of members to ask questions and express concerns about anyone—leadership included

- Safe environments for discussing spiritual confusion and doubts

- Support systems for those recovering from spiritual deception

PRACTICAL PROTECTION STRATEGIES

Strategy 1: Screening and Evaluation

Before inviting anyone to teach or speak:

- Research their background, training, and spiritual influences

- Review their published materials and recorded teachings

- Check references from other biblical churches and organizations

- Evaluate their understanding and commitment to biblical authority

Red Flags to look for:

- Training in non-Christian spiritual disciplines

- Use of New Age terminology or concepts

- Emphasis on experience over biblical truth

- Claims of special revelation or spiritual techniques

- Mixing of Christian concepts with non-biblical practices

Evaluating Curriculum and Materials:

- Review all educational materials for non-biblical content

- Research authors and publishers for spiritual background

- Test all spiritual practices against clear biblical standards

- Avoid materials that promote techniques borrowed from other religions

Strategy 2: Education and Training

Regular Discernment Teaching:

- Continued teaching on spiritual deception and discernment

- Workshops on evaluating contemporary spiritual trends

- Bible studies that address specific deceptive practices

- Training sessions for small group leaders, ministry workers, and any believers interested

Specific Training Topics:

- The difference between biblical and non-biblical meditation

- How to recognize New Age concepts in Christian packaging

- Understanding the spiritual roots of popular wellness practices

- Evaluating Christian books, conferences, and teaching materials

Age-Appropriate Education:

- Children's programs that build strong biblical foundations

- Youth ministry that addresses peer pressure and cultural spiritual trends

- Adult education that provides a sophisticated understanding of spiritual deception

- Senior adult classes that help recognize deception targeting their age group

Strategy 3: Creating Safe Spaces for Questions

Encourage Honest Inquiry:

- Regular forums where people can ask questions about spiritual practices being done by anyone in the church, including leaders, as well as outside the church

- Small group environments that welcome discussion of doubts and concerns

- Leadership availability for individual consultations about spiritual matters

- Anonymous question submission systems for sensitive topics

Responding to any Questions or Spiritual Confusion:

- Humble responses to anyone—always remembering we only "see, hear, and know in part"

- Patient, loving responses to those who have been involved in deceptive practices

- Clear biblical teaching without condemnation or shame

- Practical help for those seeking to leave deceptive spiritual practices

- Ongoing support for those recovering from spiritual deception

ADDRESSING SPECIFIC

VULNERABILITIES

Vulnerability 1: The Seeking Heart

The Challenge:

People with genuine spiritual hunger may seek satisfaction through any available means when the church fails to provide authentic spiritual depth.

The Solution:

- Provide deep, authentic spiritual experiences grounded in biblical truth

- Offer multiple opportunities for spiritual growth and development

- Create mentorship relationships that guide spiritual seeking

- Demonstrate that biblical Christianity offers the most satisfying spiritual reality

Vulnerability 2: The Wounded Soul

The Challenge:

People wounded by church experiences or life traumas may be vulnerable to alternative spiritual healing methods.

The Solution:

- Provide a SAFE place for them to talk about anything without judgement

- Provide biblical counseling and inner healing ministries

- Address church hurt and spiritual abuse honestly and thoroughly

- Offer practical support during times of crisis and difficulty

- Demonstrate Christ's love through authentic care and community

Vulnerability 3: The Intellectual Seeker

The Challenge:

Intellectually minded people may be attracted to sophisticated-sounding spiritual philosophies that seem more educated than simple biblical faith.

The Solution:

- Provide intellectually satisfying biblical teaching, digging deep into the Greek and Hebrew

- Engage with contemporary philosophical and spiritual ideas from a biblical perspective

- Connect seekers with well-trained Christian believers

- Demonstrate that biblical faith produces the greatest intellectual achievements in history

Vulnerability 4: The Culturally Influenced

The Challenge:

People immersed in secular culture may unknowingly absorb spiritual concepts that contradict biblical truth.

The Solution:

- Regular teaching of a biblical worldview and cultural analysis

- Help people recognize and evaluate cultural and spiritual influences

- Provide alternative Christian cultural expressions and activities

- Create a strong Christian community that offers belonging and identity

WHEN DECEPTION ENTERS THE CHURCH

Early Detection and Response

Warning Signs to Watch For:

- Unusual spiritual manifestations or experiences

- Teaching that contradicts the Word

- Practices borrowed from non-Christian spiritual traditions

- Emphasis on technique or experience over relationship with God

- Claims of special revelation or spiritual superiority

Immediate Response Steps:

1. **Investigation:** Carefully examine the teaching or practice against Scripture

2. **Consultation:** Seek wisdom from mature believers

3. **Prayer:** Seek God's wisdom and protection through corporate prayer and spiritual warfare

4. **Action:** Take appropriate steps to address the deception directly

Confronting Deception with Love

Approaching Deceived Individuals:

- Lead with love and concern rather than condemnation

- Provide clear biblical evidence for your concerns

- Offer support and help rather than just criticism

- Give opportunity for repentance and restoration

Addressing Deceptive Teaching:

- Respond publicly to public teaching that contradicts Scripture

- Provide clear biblical alternatives to deceptive practices

- Offer education to help people understand the biblical issues involved

- Take disciplinary action when necessary to protect the congregation

Restoration and Healing

For Those Who Have Been Deceived:

- Provide patient, loving support during the recognition and repentance process

- Offer practical help in breaking free from deceptive practices

- Connect them with others who have experienced similar freedom

- Provide ongoing training and spiritual growth opportunities

For the Congregation:

- Address any confusion or division caused by deceptive teaching

- Provide additional biblical education to strengthen discernment

- Examine church practices to prevent future deception

- Celebrate God's faithfulness in protecting and delivering His people

BUILDING LONG-TERM IMMUNITY

Generational Protection

Children and Youth Ministry:

- Build strong biblical foundations that resist later deception

- Teach age-appropriate discernment skills and spiritual warfare concepts

- Create positive spiritual experiences that satisfy spiritual hunger biblically

- Prepare young people to face spiritual challenges in the secular culture we all live in

Family Ministry:

- Equip parents to protect and train their children spiritually

- Provide resources for family devotions and biblical education

- Support homeschooling families with biblical curriculum and community

- Create family-friendly church activities that build a strong Christian community

Leadership Development:

- Train future leaders in biblical discernment and spiritual warfare

- Provide biblical education that includes contemporary spiritual challenges

- Create mentorship relationships that pass on wisdom about spiritual deception

- Develop a plan that maintains biblical fidelity across generations

Community Strength

Strong Biblical Fellowship:

- Create deep, authentic relationships that provide belonging and identity

- Develop relationships that keep everyone accountable to God—including spiritual protection

- Provide practical support during times of crisis and challenge

- Demonstrate love and unity that show the superiority of biblical community

Outreach and Mission:

- Engage in practical evangelism by demonstrating the power and truth of the gospel in daily interactions versus preaching "at" people

- Serve the community in ways that show Christ's love practically

- Support missions that spread biblical truth globally

- Provide an alternative spiritual community for those leaving deceptive practices

THE CHURCH'S CALLING

Protecting the church from spiritual deception is not just a defensive necessity—it's a calling to demonstrate the superior reality of Biblical Truth and Authentic Relationship with God.

The church that successfully builds spiritual immunity will:

Provide Authentic Spiritual Reality:

- Deep, satisfying spiritual experiences grounded in biblical truth

- A genuine community that meets human needs for belonging and purpose

- Real transformation that demonstrates the power of the gospel

- Hope and healing that surpass what deceptive spirituality offers

Maintain Biblical Fidelity:

- Unwavering commitment to Scripture as the final authority

- Clear doctrinal positions that distinguish truth from error

- Regular teaching that builds strong biblical foundations

- Leadership that prioritizes truth over cultural accommodation

Demonstrate Papa's Heart:

- Love and compassion for those trapped in spiritual deception

- Patient restoration for those who have been deceived

- Protective care for the vulnerable and spiritually immature

- Missionary heart to reach those seeking spiritual truth

Build Generational Strength:

- Strong foundations that protect future generations

- Wisdom passed down through faithful training

- Cultural engagement that maintains biblical distinctiveness

- Legacy of truth that endures through changing spiritual climates

The church's calling is clear: to be a lighthouse of Biblical Truth in a sea of spiritual deception—offering hope, healing, and authentic relationship with the One True God through Jesus Christ.

This calling requires vigilance, wisdom, courage, and above all, deep love for those whom Papa desires to set free.

Because that's what we're here for.

Setting the Captives Free.

CHAPTER TWENTY-TWO

The Masking   The Un-Masking

THE UNSEEN WORLD

What if I told you there was an Unseen World ALL Around Us?

Another dimension. Filled with angels and demons.

A NGELS WHO ARE THERE to protect us if we yield to the Lord.

And demons, ALWAYS "hiding in the wings," waiting for ANY invitation.

What if I told you the demons are constantly setting up circumstances in and around you so you'll give them permission to come in? Any permission.

What would you think or do differently from now on, when you've just found out all you had to do was SIMPLY give in and agree with their ploys?

Would you feel empowered, or would you feel scared?

Not sure. Good. You should feel both.

Empowered because now you know the rules of engagement. Scared because you finally realize what you've been up against your whole life without knowing it.

All of us were raised by the god of this world and trained by him and his demons for this very reason: To yield to him and give him full control.

As taught in the first book, it's **ALL** a matter of choice and yielding. That,

"We are a vessel to whomever we yield."

THE VEIL BETWEEN WORLDS

Scripture is clear: there's a spiritual realm that exists alongside our physical one. Most people stumble through life completely unaware of it—or worse, they dabble in it without understanding what they're really dealing with.

"For we do not wrestle against flesh and blood, but against principalities, against powers, against the rulers of the darkness of this age, against spiritual hosts of wickedness in the heavenly places." (Ephesians 6:12)

Paul isn't speaking metaphorically here. He's describing **actual beings** in an **actual dimension** with an **actual hierarchy** waging an **actual war**.

"Oh come on, Tom. This is the 21st century. We don't believe in invisible beings anymore. That's just superstitious medieval thinking."

Really?

Then explain to me why the same people who mock the idea of demons have no problem believing in "spirit guides," "higher selves," "ascended masters," "the Universe," and "energy beings."

Explain why they'll pay good money to have a psychic "channel" messages from "the other side."

Explain why they meditate to "connect with higher consciousness" but call Christians crazy for praying to God.

Same realm. Same beings. Different marketing.

WHAT THEY'RE REALLY AFTER

Here's the thing most people don't understand about demons: They need you to fulfill their destiny.

They know their ultimate destiny is going to live in hellfire for eternity with their boss, the devil. So, their current destiny is to find all they can to take with them.

Misery Loves Company.

They need you because they, like their boss, love to torture the innocent and want to destroy as many as possible because they know their time is short.

Demons crave expression as they cause destruction to the human world. They want to act out all their sadistic dreams on and through you. And to influence others through you to come along "for the ride." Before they cast you aside to die.

That's why they're constantly looking for an "in." An invitation. A door.

And they're very patient.

The Invitation They're Waiting For

Every spiritual practice we've discussed in this book—every form of Woo, every counterfeit spirituality, every mystical technique—is essentially an **invitation**.

When you empty your mind in Eastern meditation, you're sending out an invitation.

When you ask your "spirit guide" for guidance, you're sending out an invitation.

When you open yourself to "the Universe" through manifestation, you're sending out an invitation.

When you attend a séance or consult a medium, you're sending out an invitation.

When you practice "Christian yoga" while chanting Sanskrit mantras, you're sending out an invitation.

And trust me—someone always RSVPs.

"But the experiences feel so positive! So enlightening! So peaceful!"

Of course they do. At first.

You think the enemy is going to show up with horns and a pitchfork announcing, "Hi, I'm here to destroy your life?"

No. He shows up as an angel of light (2 Corinthians 11:14). Offering exactly what you think you need. Peace. Power. Purpose. Connection. Enlightenment.

The bait is always attractive. That's why it's called bait.

THE HIERARCHY OF DARKNESS

Most people have no idea how organized the enemy's kingdom is. Paul lists them in Ephesians 6: principalities, powers, rulers of darkness, spiritual hosts of wickedness in high places.

This isn't random chaos. This is a military structure.

- **Principalities** — High-ranking demonic rulers over regions, nations, territories, and denominations

- **Powers** — Authorities with specific jurisdictions and influence

- **Rulers of darkness** — Those who govern specific areas of deception and bondage

- **Spiritual hosts of wickedness** — The foot soldiers carrying out the agenda

Behind every false religion and denomination, there's a principality. Behind every addictive substance, there's a power. Behind every cultural deception, there's a ruler of darkness.

And behind every individual bondage—every person trapped in Woo, in New Age, in counterfeit spirituality—there's a host of wickedness assigned specifically to keep them blind and bound.

Your Personal Assignment

Here's something most believers don't realize: You have demons assigned to you.

NOT because you're **special**. Because you're a **threat**.

Every believer walking in relationship with the True and Living God is a threat to the enemy's kingdom. So he assigns spirits to watch you, study you, find your weaknesses, and exploit every door you open.

They know your family history.

Your generational curses.

Your personal struggles.

Your secret sins.

Your emotional wounds.

They've been watching your family for generations—as I explained in Chapter 14, they have the largest data bank on everyone who's ever lived. They know exactly which buttons to push.

"That's terrifying, Tom!"

Good. It should be.

But here's the part they don't want you to know:

They have NO power over you that you don't give them.

THE GOOD NEWS

For all their organization, all their knowledge, all their patience—demons have one massive limitation:

They need your permission.

They can tempt. They can deceive. They can suggest. They can pressure. They can harass.

But they cannot force you.

Every demonic influence in your life came through a door you opened—or that was opened for you through generational lines, trauma, or someone else's sin against you.

And every door that was opened can be closed.

Through the authority of Jesus Christ.

Through repentance and renunciation.

Through choosing to yield to Papa God instead of the god of this world.

THE REAL WAR

This is the war that's been raging since before you were born. It's the war behind every deception we've discussed in this book.

It's not about yoga versus Christianity.

It's not about New Age versus traditional religion.

It's not about meditation versus prayer.

It's about two kingdoms fighting for your allegiance.

The Kingdom of God. And the kingdom of darkness.

And you are the battleground.

The Choice Before You

EVERY single day, you make choices about who you will yield to.

EVERY thought you entertain.

EVERY practice you engage in.

EVERY belief you embrace.

EVERY door you open—or close.

You're either yielding to the True and Living God, walking under His authority and protection—or you're yielding to the god of this world, giving him access and influence.

There is NO neutral ground.

You can't ignore it. There is NO such thing as being a "happy agnostic" who believes they're "safe" not yielding directly to the enemy or the True God of the universe.

As Jesus said, "**He who is not with me is against me.**" (Matthew 12:30)

Unfortunately for those who try to ignore this truth, the enemy knows he's already WON, and it's just a matter of time before he takes you down.

EYES WIDE OPEN

If our eyes were truly opened to see the unseen world—**EVEN FOR A MOMENT**—we would **NEVER** be the same.

We would see the angels assigned to guard us.

We would see the demons assigned to destroy us.

We would see the war raging all around us every single day.

And we would finally understand why **EVERY** choice matters. Why **EVERY** yielding has consequences. **Why Papa God takes spiritual purity so seriously**.

If we ONLY knew.

If we ONLY understood the Truth.

We'd NEVER be or respond the same to ANY of this—EVER again.

So now you know.

The unseen world is real. The war is real. The choice is yours.

Who will you yield to?

CHAPTER TWENTY-THREE

CONCLUSION: THE CONTINUING BATTLE FOR TRUTH

THE ONGOING NATURE OF SPIRITUAL WARFARE

SO, NOW WHAT?

Y OU'VE MADE IT TO the end of this book.

Are you going to close these pages, nod thoughtfully, and go right back to living exactly the same way you were before?

Because that's what most people do.

They read. They agree. They even get a little fired up. And then... nothing. Back to the same old patterns. Same practices. Same compromises. Same spiritual sleepwalking.

I didn't write this book for "most people."

I wrote it for the ones who are actually willing to do something with what they've learned.

Which one are you?

THE BATTLE DOESN'T END HERE

This isn't a onetime victory.

It's a lifetime war.

The spiritual deceptions we've exposed in this book aren't going away. They're getting more sophisticated. More culturally accepted. More deeply embedded in churches. More convincing in their counterfeits. And more relentless in their pursuit of the next generation.

As spiritual deceptions become more sophisticated and culturally accepted, the church must become more discerning and biblically grounded.

This isn't optional. It's survival.

"But Tom, you're being so negative! Can't we just focus on the positive?"

Sure. While the enemy is systematically deceiving millions, let's all hold hands and sing kumbaya.

That "positive thinking" approach is exactly why the church is in the mess it's in. We've been so afraid of being "negative" that we've stopped warning people about the pit they're about to fall into.

A lifeguard who refuses to yell "Shark!" because it might upset the swimmers isn't being positive. They're being negligent.

BUT HERE'S THE GOOD NEWS

Despite the challenges, we serve a God who has **already WON** the ultimate victory over deception and spiritual darkness.

Jesus Christ has already defeated every spiritual enemy. His Truth will ultimately prevail.

Our role is to faithfully participate in His victory by:

- **Standing** firm in biblical truth regardless of cultural pressure

- **Setting** the captives free through love, truth, and spiritual authority

- **Building** spiritual immunity in ourselves and our communities

- **Passing** on these truths to future generations

The outcome is already determined. The question is whether you'll be on the winning side—not just positionally, but actively.

THE CALL TO ACTION

Every believer has a role to play in this spiritual battle.

If You're Still in Deception

Maybe you picked up this book and realized somewhere in these pages that you're the one who's been deceived.

Good. That realization is the first step to freedom.

The door to freedom stands open. Papa God loves you and desires to set you free from every form of spiritual bondage. No matter how deeply you've been involved, how much you've invested, or how long you've been deceived—freedom is possible through Jesus Christ.

You don't have to clean yourself up first. You don't have to figure it all out. You just have to be willing.

Are you willing?

"But I've been doing this for years! My whole identity is wrapped up in it!"

No, it isn't. That's a lie you've been told—and that you've told yourself.

Your identity is not in your spiritual practices. Your identity is in whose image you were created.

You were created for relationship with the True and Living God.

Everything else is a COUNTERFEIT.

If You've Already Found Freedom

Your freedom comes with responsibility.

God has set you free not just for your own benefit, but so you can help others find the same liberation. Share your testimony. Offer support to those seeking freedom. And help protect others from the deceptions you escaped.

You know what it's like on the inside. You understand the pull, the deception, the fear of leaving. You have a perspective that someone who's never been there simply doesn't have.

Use it.

If You're a Church Leader

The sheep under your care are your sacred responsibility.

Build their spiritual immunity through strong biblical teaching. Create safe spaces for honest questions. And maintain an unwavering commitment to biblical truth even when it's culturally unpopular.

Especially when it's culturally unpopular.

Because here's the hard truth: Many church leaders have been complicit in bringing deception into the church. Through ignorance, through compromise, through wanting to be "relevant."

If that's you—repent. Clean house. Start protecting your flock instead of exposing them.

For the Whole Church

We are called to be salt and light in a spiritually dark world.

Our unity in Biblical Truth, our demonstration of authentic spiritual reality, and our love for those trapped in deception will draw many living in darkness into God's marvelous Light and Truth.

This isn't about winning arguments. It's about winning souls.

This isn't about being right. It's about setting people free.

This isn't about condemning the deceived. It's about rescuing them with the same love and compassion that Papa showed us when we were lost.

THE ULTIMATE HOPE

Our hope is not in perfect discernment.

It's not in flawless understanding.

It's not in complete spiritual maturity.

Our Hope is in Jesus Christ ALONE.

He came to Set the Captives Free. And He continues that work through His people today.

As we follow Him faithfully, study His Word diligently, love others genuinely, and trust the Spirit of God completely, we participate in the greatest liberation movement in history. The ongoing work of setting the captives free and **bringing them Home to Papa's Heart**.

Again,

"The Spirit of the Lord is upon me, because He has anointed me to **proclaim good news to the poor**. He has sent me to **proclaim liberty to the captives** and **recovering of sight to the blind**, to **set at liberty those who are oppressed**, to **proclaim the year of the Lord's favor**." (Luke 4:18-19)

ONE LAST THING

I started this book by telling you I don't care if you agree with me.

I lied.

I do care.

Not because I need your validation—**but because I know what's at stake**.

I've watched people I love get pulled into spiritual deception. I've seen the destruction it causes. I've witnessed bondage that looks like freedom and darkness that Masquerades as light.

And I've seen people set free. I've watched the chains fall off. I've witnessed the moment when someone finally sees the Truth—and chooses it.

That's why I wrote this book.

Not to win an argument. Not to prove I'm right.

But because **Setting the Captives Free is what Papa does.**

And He's invited us to be part of it.

So.

The book is finished.

The question is: What will you do now?

Will you be set free?

Will you help set others free?

Will you stand for Truth in a world drowning in deception?

The battle continues.

Whose side are you on?

ABOUT THE AUTHOR

HI, I'M TOM SNOW

FIRST, LET ME INTRODUCE MYSELF

I'm a conservative Believer and not part of any organized religion or denomination. As a Jewish Christian, I believe that there is one God who created ALL; and ALL are equal in God's creation. That there is only one True Church which is the Body of Christ ~ of which ALL True Believers are a part. I believe in God's Light that dispels darkness and binarily separates Truth from lies. I believe we have not only a spiritual responsibility in the Church but also equally in the world.

In fifty-plus years, I've been tested in many ways, gone to hell and back, and lived to talk about it. Walking with the Lord is SIMPLE, it's just not EASY. The road is narrow. The works written and coming result from being humbled and learning over those many years, and still learning today, tomorrow, and until His return. My goal is to share what little I've learned along the way to help equip other believers to learn to Walk in the Anointing, then Stand in God's Authority.

While many are chasing a million different answers in a million different ways, there's only ONE. ALL the Greatest Mysteries, Wisdom, Understandings, and Secrets of God and the Universe are revealed inside ONE Simple Truth: being IN CHRIST. Hence, I want to live my life in the Presence and the Heart of the Father, Papa God.

SECOND, HERE'S WHAT I'VE DONE

I'm the retired owner of a software design company that was in business for over 45 years. I'm currently launching a new Healthy Foods Company (NaturesGoldenFire.com).

Go to Nature's Golden Fire

Introducing **GREAT TASTING** *100% Salt-Free* and *100% Sugar-Free* products for the 280 million people in the US and the 1.5 billion people in the world who need to be on "a low sodium" diet—because of heart, kidney, and high blood pressure diseases—but aren't.

I'm an engineer, inventor, entrepreneur, hunter, and fisherman; but most importantly, I love the Lord, my beautiful wife, my five children, and my eight grandchildren.

AND, I'M ALSO WRITING BOOKS AS THE LORD DIRECTS.

LEAVE A REVIEW

HOW WOULD YOU REVIEW SET THE CAPTIVES FREE TOO?

Scan to Review

How did the book affect you?

Have you been set free, are you being set free, or do you know someone who needs to be?

Be honest with yourself and review accordingly so others can be set free as well.

Thank you for reading and reviewing SET THE CAPTIVES FREE TOO.   – Tom

www.ingramcontent.com/pod-product-compliance
Lightning Source LLC
Chambersburg PA
CBHW070906130626
46555CB00001B/22